BLESSINGS FOR A BROKEN MAN

MIKE GONZALEZ

BLESSINGS FOR A BROKEN MAN

MIKE GONZALEZ

Editor: Regina Cornell

Cover Design: LUCAS Art & Design

Interior Design: Whitney Evans, SGR-P Services

Indigo River Publishing

3 West Garden Street, Ste. 352

Pensacola, FL 32502

www.indigoriverpublishing.com

Ordering Information:

Quantity sales: Special discounts are available on quantity purchases by corporations, associations, and others. For details, contact the publisher at the address above.

Orders by U.S. trade bookstores and wholesalers: Please contact the publisher at the address above.

Printed in the United States of America

Library of Congress Control Number: 2017956883

ISBN: 978-0-9990210-9-5

First Edition

With Indigo River Publishing, you can always expect great books, strong voices, and meaningful messages. Most importantly, you'll always find...words worth reading.

for Melinda

CONTENTS

1. Going Under   1
2. A Fight for the Soul   8
3. Blessings for a Broken Man   13
4. A Second Chance at Life   17
5. An Unexpected Blessing   25
6. Time to Fight   33
7. Another Dance with Death   45
8. My Daily Mantra   53
9. Mentally Broke   69
10. The Wedding   79
11. The Start of Normal   83
12. Violence of Action   93
13. Back to Work   102
14. My New Reality   108

Acknowledgments   119
Pictures of Me   121

"When your time comes to die, be not like those whose hearts are filled with fear of death, so that when their time comes they weep and pray for a little more time to live their lives over again in a different way. Sing your death song, and die like a hero going home."
   -Tecumseh

[1]
GOING UNDER

I WAS SCARED. They were going to intubate me. For almost ten years, I had been a patrol officer, and I had been around hospital emergency rooms before, so I knew what this meant. I had known things were bad, but nowhere near this bad.

My girlfriend, Melinda, and my lieutenant were at the hospital in the ICU room with me. Having been a paramedic for many years in California before becoming a police officer, my lieutenant told me I needed to let them put me under. They injected me with a sedative, but I didn't go out. I remember them attempting to place a tube down my throat. There were nurses and staff all around me. Melinda tried to tell me to calm down and relax. The memory is a blur, but somehow, certain things are so clear to me. I remember the look on Melinda's face. She looked scared. No—terrified.

I began to struggle with the nursing staff. They sent Melinda out of the room and strapped me down. People pulled at me, and someone forced my head back and mouth open. A tube was pushed down my throat. Then the pressure from the people holding me down was gone. I heard talking, and the bed I was in began to move. I could no longer move or speak, but I could see and faintly hear what was going on around me.

I was now being wheeled down the hall to what I was guessing was impending surgery. For what, I didn't know. All I knew was that I was still awake. Fear was growing in me. How could I tell these people I was still awake? I tried so hard to cry out, but nothing happened. I tried to move my arms and legs. Nothing. Lord, don't let me go into this surgery awake! We finally rounded the last corner to a room with large double doors. I remember the doors opening, and then, thankfully, I was out.

———

Around two weeks prior to this, I had started to feel tired, achy, and had a slight headache and a runny nose. I was also having trouble breathing. Typically twice a year, I would get colds that I would just fight through. I didn't go to doctors or take medication. I thought that was for weak people, and I certainly wasn't that. Hell, it had been snowing this December, and my sergeant and I still showed up for our 0500-1700 patrol shifts in short sleeves with no jackets because we were tough guys.

This time, my sickness didn't get better. I remember trying to sweat out the sickness in a late-night weightlifting session in the garage on a Saturday night before work the following day. I felt weak and wondered why I couldn't get all my reps in on my incline press. I verbalized my frustration to my girlfriend Melinda, got cleaned up, and went to bed. I woke up the next morning around 0340 hours to get ready to be at work for my 0500 hour briefing Sunday morning. I wasn't feeling well, but I got dressed and drove in to work. After the briefing, my sergeant told me that I didn't look good, which was unusual because my sergeant was probably the toughest no-nonsense guy at the police department. He was the SWAT sergeant, never called in sick, and hated having his troops call in sick. He seemed concerned with the way I looked, but I went out on the streets and completed my twelve-hour shift anyway.

Monday, I woke up feeling horrible. I knew something wasn't quite right. I had recently been to the local emergency clinic for our department physical. Since they already had all of my information on file, I thought I could get in, grab some medication, get out quick, and be good to go for work on Wednesday. I spoke with an intake nurse, explaining my symptoms and telling her I thought I might have the flu. I was assured I didn't have the flu but, more than likely, had an upper respiratory infection. I was given medication and sent home. Wednesday came around, and I still didn't feel right. I pushed through my patrol shift and went home afterward. Usually on Monday, Wednesday, Friday, and Sunday nights, I went straight from work to the gym where I train in Dallas. I was part of a competitive powerlifting team and never missed a workout. It would be an ass chewing from the guys if I did. Nevertheless, I sent a text out to everyone, took the chewing, and went home to get some rest.

0340 hours came around quickly, and I reluctantly rolled out of bed and got dressed for my patrol shift. If I had felt horrible the day before, I felt like I had been run over by six or seven trucks this morning. I remember getting into my pickup and heading to work. I started to feel dizzy and called my sergeant, telling him I was trying to drive to work but wasn't feeling right. I told him I would continue on to work, hit the streets, and if I felt worse I would leave. He was fine with this. In the past, I would always try to at least show up to work and make an effort before leaving. This morning, I didn't even make it to the police department. I ran a red light—I never saw it—and started weaving all over the road. I called my sergeant, told him what was going on, and headed back home. I feared I would cause an accident if I continued and feared more that I would wreck a squad car if I did make it to work.

After parking my pickup in the driveway at home, I got out and walked about two steps before falling down in the front yard. I wasn't sure what had happened. Maybe I had just lost my balance or tripped over something. Actually, I was dizzy from lack of oxygen. I had no idea at the time, but my oxygen levels were already dangerously low. I made it inside the house and lay down. I slept for a couple of hours and then got up and drove to the same e-clinic as before to see if they could tell me what the heck was going on. I remember them telling me that their x-ray machine was broken, but they felt that I had double walking pneumonia. I was given medication for this and headed back home. I remember feeling proud that I had something as serious-sounding as double walking pneumonia, yet I was still trying to power through work.

Yeah, I was an idiot, to say the least.

Two days later, I was back at the e-clinic. I was worse now, and the medication they had given me was not putting a dent in my symptoms. I was still having trouble breathing, I couldn't sleep, I was achy all over, and I had so much mucus dripping out of my nose I was going through an entire box of tissues a day. This time, their x-ray machine was actually working, so they took some readings. Due to my complaint of not being able to breathe very well, they also checked my oxygenation level and found that it was in the 70s—dangerously low. A normal level would be in the mid- to high 90s. Too much time spent with low oxygen levels in the 70s can lead to brain damage. I was immediately put on oxygen and taken to one of their exam rooms. A while later, a doctor came in and told me that I did, in fact, have double walking pneumonia and that my condition was bad enough that they recommended hospitalization. I responded that this wouldn't be possible because I had things to do, so I requested that I be given medication and released. The doctor insisted that my condition was very serious and I needed to be transported to a hospital immediately. I was able to talk them into letting me drive myself because I didn't want to incur the expense of an ambulance ride. It was not their protocol, but since the hospital was only a couple of blocks away, they let me drive. I got into my pickup and began driving to the small hospital that had been recommended. I remember not being able to react quickly enough to things around me. Multiple times, I hit curbs and almost drove over the median trying to get into the parking lot of the hospital. My mind was starting to fail me, and I felt like I was trying to think through a thick fog. Nothing was functioning normally. My body just wasn't responding.

Upon arriving at the hospital, I made my way to the check-in area and told the staff about my condition, and they showed me to my room. I thought I was starting to feel okay again...maybe things weren't so bad. But then things started to change. Once in the hospital room, I was put back on oxygen. Melinda and one of my buddies from the gym came to visit and brought me food. Food is always a good way to make me feel better. I had no appetite, though. I wanted nothing to do with any food. I started to feel out of it again. I still didn't realize how serious things were until, after running a battery of tests on me, my doctor came in and told me that my condition was grave. I was sitting in my hospital bed when the doctor walked into my room. He stood on my left side and got straight to the point.

"Mr. Gonzalez, I have been going over the results of the tests we ran on you, and from what I'm seeing, you might not make it. Mr. Gonzalez, you might not live past tomorrow," he told me.

What he might have said after this I don't recall. His first two sentences, however, made a big impact on me, and I remember it like it was yesterday. I remember the way I felt: part of me was confused by what he had said. I had never been told anything like this before. Not live past tomorrow? I was confused. Not make it? I had to return to work on Monday. Hell, I had a class of recruits to teach! A few days before, I was fine, and now I am being told I might die?!

I was also angry. What a horrible bedside manner this guy had! His face was a blank mask, showing no expression—no look of empathy, no look of thoughtful concern. I wasn't looking to be coddled like a baby, but hell, if you're gonna tell a young guy that he's going from being healthy to being dead in a day or so, you might want to show some kind of compassion. If anyone had been in the room with me at the time, I'm sure they would have grilled him with questions. After a few moments, he walked out, and I was left lying in that bed, still trying to fully process what was happening. Have you ever imagined what it would be like to go to your doctor for a routine checkup only to be told that you have terminal cancer? Up until this point in my life, I couldn't have fathomed what that must be like emotionally and mentally. Well, I guess I got my answer. I was numb and didn't believe him. I was just sick, that's all. I wasn't going to die. I couldn't die. I had too many things to do.

A short time later, a nurse came in and told me she was going to give me a cocktail of medications created by the doctor to help me sleep. A good night's sleep would be good. I hadn't slept well in a while and thought maybe this was just the thing to get me back on the road to healing and the heck out of this place. I was given the drugs and remember feeling loopy as hell. I was singing made-up songs and saying very strange things. Melinda looked at me with concern. She wasn't laughing like she typically would if I were acting goofy. Normally, she loved it when I acted goofy, not like a tough guy cop. Not even a smile from her now, though. A short time later, I finally fell asleep.

I awoke some hours later to a room full of concerned people. Apparently, the hospital staff almost couldn't wake me. When they finally did, I awoke to find Melinda and my sergeant and lieutenant standing in my room. The doctor was telling them that my condition had degraded even more and I needed to be transported to a bigger hospital because they could no longer help me. With only one bed available at another local hospital, they had an ambulance on its way to get me, and if I didn't leave now, I was told, I might not make it. Shortly, I was loaded into the ambulance, and the trip began. It should have been only a five-minute drive, but the ambulance driver got lost. I remember wanting to tell them how to get to the hospital because this was my patrol beat, but I decided to let them figure it out. For some reason, I thought it was funny. The severity of the situation still hadn't sunk in fully. A few days earlier, I had been working the streets. Now, I was being transported by ambulance to a hospital because of my "grave condition," as the doctor had put it. Certainly, I felt off, but not like I was close to death. Of course, who among us really knows what it's like to be on death's door due to a sudden sickness? Dangerous situations while on patrol? Sure, I knew about that. But quickly falling ill and just dropping dead? No, I still couldn't wrap my head around it. Surely, at the larger hospital they would find the cause of all my issues, treat me, and I'd be on my way home.

Once we arrived at the hospital, I was wheeled into the ICU unit and intubated a short time later.

[2]

A FIGHT FOR THE SOUL

I WAKE UP FACEDOWN. *I can hear voices around me; they sound foreign. I also hear what sounds like people moving around me quickly as if they are running. I try to pick my head up off the ground, but it won't move. I try and try, but nothing happens. What is going on? Why can't I move? I try to really concentrate. This time, I am able to move my head just enough to the right to be able to see what is going on around me. I am at the local church where I work uniformed security jobs for Sunday services. The preacher at this particular church is known worldwide, and at times, people have to be removed from the property due to erratic and unsafe behavior, to say the least. I collect myself enough to realize I am in the main sanctuary of the church. About twenty feet away from me, four men stand, holding guns and yelling. People are running from the sanctuary in all directions.*

I have to act. I have to get up and stop the threat these men pose before anyone is hurt. I can't move, though. Why can't I move? One of the men comes over to me. Standing over me with a gun in his hand, he laughs and tells me I will die today. I struggle with everything I have to reach the gun I know is on my hip. I must be back at work in uniform. Something must have happened, causing me to lose time. I don't remember being sick and going into the hospital. Time has skipped somewhere for me. I am at my part-time security job on Sunday at the church, not in the hospital. And now, I am in an active-shooter situation, and I am losing. The back of my head aches. One of them must have hit me over the head to knock me out. Maybe I was paralyzed somehow, too. No part of my body works. The strange man puts the gun to my head... I black out.

Again, I awake. How much time has passed? I have no idea. It could have been a minute; it could have been days. Once more, I am facedown and cannot see or more. I feel gravel on my face and all around me this time. What is going on? I struggle again, but again, nothing happens. The back of my head still aches. As before, I hear people talking around me but can't move to see what is going on. The voices seem strange to me—not like a foreign language, just strange-sounding. They are loud but, at the same time, distant. Repeatedly, I struggle to move. Finally, my head moves to the side, and I can see. I am by a set of railroad tracks. What am I doing here? I'm not at work this time. I see a man walking towards me. I feel threatened, not knowing why—maybe because I can't move. I have never felt completely vulnerable before, and I panic. As the man approaches, I don't recognize him as the man from the church, but the feeling is the same. He holds a revolver in his hand. He tells me I will die and points the gun at my head. I can't even speak to respond to him. Again, I black out.

Over the next two and half months this would be my reality. To me, there was not shift in time or movement from being awake to being asleep or to being dead. It all melded into one. One smooth transition. What I was experiencing to me was real. As real as any experience I've had in my life.

I don't speak about what happened to me during this time much. It's not because I can't remember what happened. It's a time and collection of memeories and experiences that are burned into my mind and will be forever. On the one hand, things that I experienced were both the very worst and terrifiying things I have every seen or heard but they were also the most beautiful and overwhelmingly joyful experiences I will ever have. Telling of each individual scenario (best way I can describe them) would not do them justice. Nor would they properly convey the message that I feel was meant behind each one.

There is also the issue of time. Time did not work as I know it does here. To me, this period of time lasted much longer than I was in a coma. One thing I can say with certaintly though is I know the difference betwen the experiences I had while sedated and heavily medicated and the times I was dead. One thing I know for sure is there was a struggle occurring for my soul. The things I saw during this time were not drug endossed. They were a product of how I had lived my life. I thought I was a good person. I thought I had done most things right. Good enough to go to heaven I had thought. I saw no bright light with a comforting feeling. What I saw was a a struggle for my soul. I was being pulled by both sides. I spent a good deal of this time running. Running from demons. Nothing was sugar coated during this time. Nothing was disguised. I was being pulled at. Things trying to pull me back with them. I was terrified and I almost gave up. I called out for help. I finally called for God to save me and he answered my calls.

These things are real. I know many people think they have an idea of what is going to happen when they die. Believers or not, they think they know. Most have no idea.

I am now in blinding sunlight in what appears to be a bright red desert. The wind is churning, and thin clouds seem to touch the ground. Or is it sand blowing, appearing like clouds? I'm not sure, but it is a violent place. No longer am I in heaven. I am running, running at full speed. I look over my shoulder and see what I can only describe as evil behind me in the fog of the red desert—creatures coming after me snarling, grunting, yelling. As I try to get away, I am terrified. I look in front of me for shelter, but there is nowhere safe to run, only empty red landscape. How will I get away? I begin to pray, pray for help in the impending fight with these monsters, these demons. I concentrate again like I did in the underground facility. I cry out for help. As I'm running, I look to my left and see warriors. I look now to my right, and again I see warriors. They are not scared; they are not running. They are prepared for battle. I stop and look at them and no longer feel fear. I know immediately that they are the answer to my prayers. They are here to protect me. How can I feel fear with this army at my side? I turn and look back at the evil creatures rushing towards me. I now face them, and I run towards them. By my side, the warriors raise their arms and run with me, and as we prepare for the impact, we have no fear, only a sense of purpose. To be brave not scared, to not be afraid but proud to meet these demons head on and fight instead of running: that is our purpose. We are now a single unit rushing towards the evil that wants to engulf us. I brace for the impact and then... Once more, things go black.

I'm back in the church sanctuary, standing this time and in uniform. The gunman is standing in front of me again, along with three other men with guns just behind him. He levels his gun in my direction and pulls the trigger. The gunfire is not loud, but the impact is tremendous. I am hit three times in the right side of my chest; I fall. The pain is immense. I look up at the gunman as I grab my side, waiting for the final gunshot that will surely end my life. As I look at him, out of the corner of my eye I see something moving. I see four officers appear from behind me. They have the same look on their faces as the warriors in the desert had. They have no fear in their eyes. They are ready for the battle. The officers level their guns towards the four gunmen and fire. The gunmen go down in a heap, dead.

I am lying on my side in great pain, preparing for death. I can feel the life leaving my body. The officers stand around me and smile. One of them speaks: "You have nothing to worry about anymore. We will take care of you. You are already saved." I look up at them, not quite knowing what to say. Then, the officer speaks again: "When you're ready, you can go back." "Back where?" I ask. They smile and say nothing. I am getting dizzy now, and things are going dark. The officers continue to stand over me, smiling...

[3]

BLESSINGS FOR A BROKEN MAN

I DON'T REMEMBER the exact moment when I woke up. Everyone wants to know what it was like and how I felt. Was I thankful? Upset? Happy? The reality was that I was so heavily sedated it took weeks for me to fully wake up. Things were hazy and disjointed for a while. Officially, I was awake, but I was still not completely aware yet.

When I finally awoke, I discovered that I had been in a coma for almost three months. During that time, I spent weeks in a RotoProne bed. I was given last rites twice, and I underwent a life-saving surgery performed by a young doctor when countless others refused to try due to the more-than-high expectancy that I would not make it through the surgery alive. I received a police escort to a special heart hospital where I underwent many more surgeries, most of which were conducted in my hospital room because my body was so frail and weak that I couldn't make the trip down the hall to the operating room without flat-lining. I received fifty-six blood transfusions and was on ECMO (a heart and lung bypass system) and survived longer than anyone else in history at the time. I was on complete life-support and almost lost my right arm and left leg due to blood clots. There was a chance I would never talk again due to possible damage to my vocal cords from all of the tubes down my throat, and it was assumed that I would either be mentally deficient or a vegetable for the rest of my life. I had scars all over my body from the surgeries as well as the different machines that were attached to my body. Part of my hair was missing because of the ECMO lines running over my head, and a chunk from the tip of my nose was also gone. (I was told I asked for a mirror at some point, but everyone agreed that I shouldn't see myself in the condition I was in. Mentally, I might break, and I needed to stay focused if I was going to make it through all of this.) I had gone into the hospital at 270 pounds of muscle. Now, I lay in bed a skeleton of myself at around 170 pounds.

Then there was the damage to my heels. When I was in a coma in the first hospital, I was placed in a RotoProne bed. A RotoProne bed is a device that rotates the patient from side to side and from being facedown to face-up so the internal organs don't flatten out from being in a stationary position all the time. You are locked in what, to me, looks like a shell with openings throughout like holes in Swiss cheese so the patient can still be accessed for treatment. Your head is immobilized, and you are basically locked in. Apparently, there is a height limit, and at 6'3," I was at the top end of that limit. My heels were dug in so tightly at the base and I was in it for so long that it opened up giant sores on both of my heels that got so big you could have fit golf balls inside of them. Now that it appeared I would survive, staff started to work on the less critical issues like the huge sores on my heels. This took many treatments consisting of cutting out the dead tissue and then wrapping my heels. Of course, I was nowhere near being able to walk, so this wasn't too much of an inconvenience for me. I had also developed a large bedsore on my lower back, almost to the bone, that required routine cleaning and bandaging. Because the wounds were so deep and most of the nerves were dead I didn't feel much pain, but I knew as they got better the pain would increase. This ordeal began when the double pneumonia progressed into acute respiratory distress syndrome (ARDS), eventually causing my lungs to stop working. Additionally, my kidneys and heart failed as well. My body wasn't responding to any treatment, and the next and final step would be to shut down the life-support machines and allow me to die. Doctors checked my brain function as well, which had all but stopped. Twice, all of my family, friends, and co-workers were told to come to the hospital and say goodbye to me because I wouldn't last the night. I have seen pictures from this time. My small room was filled with flowers, balloons, pictures, and written prayers. The hospital was flooded by police officers, firefighters, gym buddies, family, and friends. This was to be my time to die. But I didn't die. My body kept pushing one day at a time, beating the odds laid out by the doctors. Everyone stayed by my side in support of me and my family, who were struggling.

My prognosis had worsened drastically. I went from being a person who was sick and near death that people were trying to save, to being a person that might be in a coma on life-support long-term. What kind of quality of life is that? The questions had to be asked about what was going to happen to me if I didn't start to come around. Would I be kept in a coma-like state for a few more months? A few years? What was the plan? It was something my family had to consider. Then one day, for no medically-explainable reason, my body started to work again. My kidneys started to function again, as did my heart. All of my vital numbers started to go up and up and up. The staff member who was watching the machines had to call in a doctor because he thought the machines were malfunctioning. They took a reading on the machines and couldn't believe what they were seeing. My body was coming back! My organs were starting to work again. They gave it ten minutes and checked the machines again to make sure there hadn't been a false reading. Again, my numbers continued to rise. They continued to check the machines over and over again for at least an hour to make sure, but the machines were reading correctly. My body was coming back to life. It was starting to heal itself. My broken body was coming back to life, and for no medical reason. It was a true blessing and miracle.

[4]

A SECOND CHANCE AT LIFE

I'M NOT sure how I got through the initial phase of coming to
grips with what had happened. I don't remember anyone sitting
down with me and explaining what I had gone through; why I
was hooked up to so many machines, why I couldn't talk, why I
couldn't move. It was all a blur, almost like when I was going
through my experiences while in a coma. I accepted my circumstances as reality and tried to figure out how best to deal with the
situation. For me, everything happening to me in the coma had
been reality. I had no concept of being in a coma, or that what I
was experiencing wasn't real. At the time, it was all real to me.
Now, I was simply in yet another situation that I had to work
through.

I was hooked up to a ventilator via a tracheostomy in the front
of my neck. Basically, a hole had been cut in my neck through
which a tube was inserted. This device did my breathing for me. I
was still in such poor condition that if this had been turned off I
would have died. While I was on the ventilator I could not eat,
drink, or speak. I distinctly remember the part about not being

able to drink. I was so thirsty it was unimaginable! All I wanted in the world was to get a drink of ice-cold water. I motioned for a drink of water to everyone I could see but was denied every time. I've never felt an urge like I had for a drink. It was maddening and miserable! Everyone around me was under strict orders, though, not to give me any liquids. If I drank something, it would go straight to my lungs and kill me.

I was told about a patient who convinced a friend to bring him a large fountain drink from a nearby convenience store. After drinking it one evening, he was dead the next morning. This didn't persuade me, though. I had never felt anything like this before. The hospital staff tried to minimize how miserable the experience was for me by giving me tiny sponges soaked in water on the end of sticks to suck on a few times a day. These looked like small suckers. Unfortunately, they didn't provide much relief. I remember trying to suck every last drop of water out of the sponges. They were so small, though, that the insignificant amount of water they could absorb evaporated just after hitting my tongue.

During one of the day shifts, a young nursing assistant was shadowing my nurse. The nurse left for a short period of time, leaving the two of us alone in my room. I quickly motioned to the nursing assistant for a cup of water. Apparently, he hadn't been told that drinking could kill me, so he quickly and politely drew a cup of water from the sink in my room. I was so weak at this stage I couldn't lift my arms to my face, let alone hold a cup to my mouth to drink. I opened my mouth, hoping he would quickly pour the water down my throat. Just as he was about to, the nurse came back into the room. She quickly made a bee line for the cup and knocked it from his hand, spilling it on the floor. Oh, I was so close! The nurse was angry with me for trying to trick the nursing assistant, and rightfully so. But I was so close...so close!

On another occasion, I begged my girlfriend to get me a small cup of water after the nurse had left my room. I was pleading with her and crying for her to hurry up and get the water. I could tell she was in a panic, and for a second, she thought about complying. I was being selfish and playing on her emotions, but I wanted something to drink that badly. She wanted to help me but knew if she did I could die. I can only imagine how it must have felt to see me like a child in bed crying, not being able to talk, motioning for water that she knew would take the pain away but would eventually kill me. I feel bad about putting her in that position.

Then the day finally came, the day I was allowed to switch from sponges to my first real drink of water. The staff came in and asked me what I wanted for my first drink. Without hesitation, I told them that I wanted a large ice-cold bottle of fruit punch Gatorade®. They laughed at me and told me that might be a bit strong for my first drink, so they offered me cold water with small chucks of ice. I quickly agreed that this would be fine. I had to have someone hold the cup for me as I drank because I was still too weak. I drank every bit of that cup of water and then ate the ice. It wasn't too long after that when they brought me fruit punch Gatorade®. It was great, too! I still remember what it felt like to be that thirsty and literally dreaming about taking a drink of water. To this day, every drink I take seems amazing to me still, and the ability to drink anything I want to drink is also a great freedom that I no longer take for granted.

Meal time was another hurdle to get over. Nowhere near as bad as wanting water, it was miserable in its own way. I was hooked up to a feeding tube, and a few times a day, a bag of mush attached to the end of the tube would deliver food straight into my stomach. The woman from food services was nice enough. Coming into my room, she would joke, saying she had a nice, big, juicy steak for me for dinner.; But it was never anything other than a strangely-colored bag of mushy liquid. It held off the pain of hunger but wasn't good for much else. I wasn't awake too often during this time, but when I was awake, there was a television on in front of me. Seeing the commercials for all of the new offerings at the fast-food restaurants made my mouth water. Oh, what I would have given for a Subway® sandwich, McDonald's® hamburger, or some Taco Bell®!!

Another challenge was not being able to talk. I was too weak to write, so everyone around me had to read my lips. Not being trained lip readers, this wasn't the easiest thing for them. I remember feeling great frustration during this time. Sometimes, I would have four or five people around my bed all trying to guess what I was saying. Many times, they could understand me, but sometimes they could not. I would get so frustrated I would just close my eyes and try to fall asleep. You cannot imagine how removed from the world you feel when you can't talk. I felt like I was trapped in the shell of my body, watching the world go by me, not able to interact. It was also scary. What if I needed something? What if I needed help? I was so weak from not moving for three months that I couldn't make a fist or lift my arms, let alone bang on something or throw something to get someone's attention. The more consciousness I gained the more scared I became.

Somehow, they were able to attach a speaking device to the tracheostomy so I could communicate. The staff had some trepidation, though, because they thought my vocal cords might possibly have been damaged due to how long I had had tubes down my throat. There was a possibility I might not be able to speak. Things still weren't sinking in so well for me. Everyone looked worried, but I wasn't thinking about it like they were—I just wanted the device put in my neck so I could finally speak!

Early one morning, staff members came into my room and

told me they were going to try the device. The tube I originally had in my throat had been replaced with a different tube, and where the original tube had been was just a hole covered by bandages. They removed the bandages and inserted the speaking device. I was asked to try it out. Reverting back to police work, I did a radio mic check for them: "Testing—1, 2, 3, 4, 5. 5, 4, 3, 2, 1." I was waiting to hear "transmission clear," but I just got blank stares and then smiles. They told me that was great, but they really just wanted to hear me say hello. Oh, well. I could communicate again, and I was so excited!

Once a week, I looked forward to a visit from a pastor who would spend a small amount of time by my bedside speaking with me. He would pray over me, and during this time, I felt comforted. One particular day, the pastor came in and began to talk. Little did he know, on this day, I would finally respond. He looked shocked when I spoke. He was the first person I remember talking to after I woke up. I don't remember what we talked about, but I remember being so thankful to be able to talk again! While speaking with the pastor, my girlfriend Melinda walked in. The look of shock on her face was priceless. No one had told her that we were going to try out the speaking device, so she was clueless as she came into the room. I wanted to surprise her when she came in, but she caught me in mid-conversation with the pastor, so that surprise was out the door. It was a good moment, though, and she was so happy.

The only negative aspect of the speaking device: no one could get me to shut up. I wanted to talk to everyone. I didn't take into account how draining talking to people would be to me. I was so weak that if I talked for too long I would be so exhausted and I would have to sleep and recover. One particularly busy day, I must have spoken to visitors for hours, and the next day, I could hardly stay awake—it had worn me out that much.

Something I do remember very clearly was my first solid meal! Although I could not wear my speaking device while I ate, drank, or slept, at least I could finally eat and drink. Although a giant steak would have been nice, I was advised that I might want to start off with something light to make sure my stomach could handle it. Contrary to stereotypically bad hospital food, the hospital I was in when I woke up had an outstanding kitchen and menu. I began with a grilled cheese sandwich, tomato soup, and a red sports drink. I was in heaven! It was the best meal I can ever remember having. In fact, every meal after that was amazing. People also brought in everything that I was seeing on TV commercials and wanting from all the local fast-food restaurants, in addition to what I was ordering from the hospital kitchen. Although I could only eat small amounts before falling back asleep from exhaustion, the first few bites I was able to get in were great!

It is hard to believe how quickly our muscles can atrophy. Before getting sick, I was a competitive powerlifter and was very strong and in great shape. During my time in a coma, I lost one hundred pounds, leaving me too weak to raise my arms, hold my head up, or do just about anything. I couldn't even shift myself from one side to the other in bed. So to sit up, even with the assistance of the motorized bed, and try to eat was a workout in itself. I remember feeling like I was starving and having food brought in and put on a tray that overhung the bed at my waist. The bed would be moved into a sitting position, and I would immediately begin to get light-headed. My body would start to shift from one side to the other, and my head would start to sag like a baby's. Someone would have to try and feed me quickly before I became too weak and the bed had to be lowered. It was a horrible feeling. I was so hungry, but exhaustion from sitting upright would take over, and literally, I would have to lay flat and take a nap. Without the food I would be too weak to recover, but sitting up to eat the food wore me out. Although food tasted great, it was a misery trying to complete a meal.

Throughout my stay, I had a huge support system in the police department. They posted a uniformed officer outside my door 24 hours a day. Some of these people I had never met before, but most I had worked with. No matter who they were, they always showed great respect and gave kind words to my family. At the second hospital, when doctors didn't think I would make it through the night, I was told there were many officers there. I really wish I could have seen that. The support for my family must have been unbelievable. Officers brought food and drinks to my loved ones and tried to make the process as easy as they could for them. They really made sure they were kept comfortable at the hospital, or at least as comfortable as you can be in a place like that.

After I was transported to a third hospital and had woken up, a staff member who was not completely familiar with my case asked me who I was and why I was so important and given so much attention. I told her I was just a simple patrol officer. She looked shocked. She said she had thought either I was the chief of police or some really bad convict that they had to keep watch over. The situation must have looked pretty strange to anyone who didn't know the details. I was even told that a very famous musician who had been at this same hospital on the same floor a few months prior to my stay hadn't gotten the kind of treatment I was receiving. Upon leaving the hospital, similar comments were made by the medics transporting me to the rehabilitation facility. Apparently, they had once transported a former president from a hospital in the area, and my departure was just about as secure as his had been.

As people visited me, many tears were shed by big, strong cops, and many stories were told by giant powerlifting buddies about how things had changed in their lives from watching me go through everything so far with my illness. People's lives were changing for the better. They were seeing the power of prayer and God firsthand. There was no medical explanation for why I survived. I should have died ten times over, but I didn't. I should have been a shell of myself, but I wasn't, and I'm not. I shouldn't be able to write this right now, but I am.

[5]
AN UNEXPECTED BLESSING

THE MOST IMPORTANT person to me throughout my illness and recovery was my girlfriend (now wife), Melinda. Melinda and I met a few months prior to my illness when I went into the veterinary clinic where she worked. She caught my eye the second I saw her. She was in a pair of scrubs with her hair pulled back, looking absolutely beautiful. I had cut my finger, and she noticed it was bleeding and asked if I wanted a bandage. Although normally, I wouldn't have worried about it, I guess I saw this as an opportunity to talk to her. I have always been horrible at "talking to women." How guys talk girls into liking them is still a mystery to me. Either girls liked me or they didn't. There wasn't much I could do about it. Still, I had to at least try to talk to her and see what kind of response I got. Thank God I did.

She took me back to where they kept medical supplies, quickly located a bandage, and put it on my finger. I remember making a comment about how I was thankful for her help because I was a delicate guy. I figured, as usual, I had failed to impress when she didn't give even a hint of a response, let alone a smile. I left after this, but when I had to return around thirty minutes later, Melinda wasn't up front like she had been. The manager was, though, and they told me that Melinda thought I was very attractive. I couldn't believe it! I didn't know what to say. To think—this gorgeous woman thought that I was attractive—it blew me away. Sheepishly, I left my number with the manager to give to Melinda. The phone number, however, didn't make it into her hands. It went into a tip jar on the counter. For the next few hours, I was on a high of confidence from what Melinda had said about me. I doubted, though, that she would ever call or text. I was right to a certain extent. Days went by, then weeks, then months. I all but forgot about Melinda. I chalked it up to nothing more than an attractive woman who had made a nice comment about me, and that was where I left it. At least I had the memory of the excitement of the encounter. It wasn't my personality to follow a woman around trying to get her attention. Like I said, either they liked me or they didn't. I just wasn't good at games.

About six months later, I was working the day shift at the police department and was sitting in my squad car in the parking lot by the sally port writing an arrest report. As I typed away on my laptop, my cell phone chimed indicating that I had received a text message. When I saved the document I was working on and checked my phone, I didn't recognize the number. It wasn't unusual to get a phone call from a number I didn't recognize, but not a text message. As I opened the message, I still figured it was someone with the wrong number.

The message read, "I'm not sure if you remember me, but you came into my clinic a few months ago. I just wanted to say hi."

I sat and thought for a minute, and then it hit me. It was that cute woman from the vet clinic from months earlier! I sat and thought for some time but couldn't remember her name. I didn't want to respond back that I didn't know who she was, so I quickly did some research on the clinic on my computer and found her.

"Melinda?"

She messaged back that she couldn't believe that I remembered her. Of course, I remembered her. How could I forget the beautiful woman who bandaged my finger? I felt like a little kid, as excited as I was that she finally responded!

We slowly began to text each other and talk and finally met for a quick lunch during the week. I took her to a Vietnamese restaurant close by that I loved. She was on her lunch break and didn't have much time. I couldn't believe how comfortable I felt with her from the very beginning. Our conversation flowed back and forth so well it was like we had known each other for a long time already. Before I knew it, we had blown past the time allowed for her lunch break. I quickly paid for the meal, hurried back to my pickup, and drove her back to the clinic. Once more, I felt like a little kid. Not only was this beautiful woman with a successful career actually interested in me, but we got along so well, too. I couldn't have asked for anything else.

As time went on, we talked more and more on the phone. One evening, we lost track of time so badly that I noticed the sun coming up through my window. How can a person be on the phone that long? I'll probably get in trouble for this, but...I had to call in sick to work that day. There was no way I could work a twelve-hour shift on patrol after being up all night. It was completely worth it, though. I fell asleep with a smile on my face that morning.

Melinda was different than me. She was my opposite, personality-wise. She was outgoing, upbeat, and always looking for a new adventure. She was such an amazing person to be around. It seemed like anything was possible with her. We went on trips together almost every month—nothing major, maybe just driving a few hours and staying in a hotel somewhere. We would explore backroads, looking for old abandoned buildings that she had an obsession with exploring. We spent hours playing with dogs at the local shelter to give them some enjoyment. She took me to hole-in-the-wall restaurants, and we ate food that I had never heard of in my life. She even took me to get my first pair of boots. All of these things might seem normal to a lot of people, but for me it was all completely new and exciting. Melinda gave me confidence and a more positive outlook on life.

Once, when we went out to eat lunch, I reached in my back pocket for my wallet so I could pay the bill. I was embarrassed when I heard a loud ripping sound. The back pocket of my old jeans had torn. When I met Melinda, I had one pair of jeans, one pair of cargo pants, two pairs of gym shorts, three polo shirts, and a handful of t-shirts, mainly from the gym. I had never worried too much about fashion or clothes before. Heck, I had worn a uniform for the last ten years, so why should I worry about clothes?

I also remember going to meet her family for the first time. We stopped off at a restaurant on the way, and I went to the bathroom to wash my hands. As I stood there looking at myself in the mirror, for the first time, I noticed how my clothes looked. My polo was too small and too short for my frame. I was again embarrassed. What would her family think of me, looking like this? Then again, why would she want to be with someone like me? Melinda was very well put together. She had a great sense of fashion and was dressed like a knockout. When I commented on my shirt, of course, she told me I looked just fine. Meeting her family went well, but back at work a day later, I was still feeling embarrassed about my clothes. I guess Melinda could tell it really bothered me, so the next day when she got off of work early, she went to the store and purchased an entire new wardrobe for me: new t-shirts, pants, shorts, polos, and some nice button-up shirts. When I went to her place that day after work, she had everything laid out on the bed for me. I couldn't believe what she had done. No one had ever done anything like that for me before, and she did it without even being prompted. It was just the type of person she is—always thinking about me and always trying to do something nice for me. It blew me away.

Our relationship moved fast. I moved in with her a short time later. We were living in the apartment she had when I met her, but I hated living there. With constant parties in the complex and drunks all over the place, I desperately wanted to move into a house in a quiet, relaxed area. Two weeks before I went into my coma, we closed on a house in a quiet neighborhood north of Dallas. It was perfect. Within the first two days, due to Melinda's obsessive-compulsive disorder, the entire place was decorated and set up. For months, she had been purchasing items for the house and putting them in a storage unit. Everything had its own place and fit perfectly.

About a week or so before Melinda and I moved into the house, she asked for phone numbers of the important people in my life in case anything ever happened to me. I am a very private person, especially about my personal life. I don't talk about relationships with people, and Melinda was worried that she would have no one to call if I got injured at work. I gave her maybe four phone numbers and shared her number with my close friends. Thank God I did this. After I was sent to the first hospital from the emergency clinic, Melinda was the first one there. One of my weightlifting buddies was the next, followed closely by two supervisors from work. It was amazing how she got along with everyone and how well everyone got along with her. She was the last person I saw before I went into the coma, and I was so thankful she was still by my side when I finally woke up.

After I woke up from my coma and started to get a grasp on things and began to understand just how severe my condition had been, I was amazed Melinda had stayed with me. She was there every day and night while I was in the first two hospitals. When medical staff told her I would die and I was given last rites, she was there. The second time I was given last rites, she was there again. Those were my first two brushes with death. She was there for my third and saved my life.

Sitting by my side, Melinda was alone with me in my hospital room. I was facedown in the RotoProne bed and had the ventilator attached to the front of my throat. As Melinda sat with me, she suddenly heard a "pop" and then the sound of gushing air. She looked up at the monitors at my bedside and saw the oxygen level numbers quickly falling. She didn't know what to do, but she quickly figured out that one of my oxygen tubes had come loose and I was not getting oxygen. She sat panicked, not sure what to do. Why wasn't someone rushing in? Why wasn't an alarm sounding? She knew she had to compose herself and do something quickly or I would die right there. Thinking fast on her feet, she knelt down beside the bed and saw a tube on the floor that was the source of the gushing air sound. She looked again at the numbers, and they were still dropping. Still no one was coming to help and no alarms were going off. Thank God she didn't panic or run for help. She found the device and saw that it was supposed to be connected into my neck. She has since told me that she was scared out of her mind. What if she didn't connect the tube correctly and then staff came in and couldn't save me because she had messed something up? What if someone never came in, though, and she did nothing and I died anyway? She took the tube off the floor, found where the oxygen tube was supposed to connect in the front of my neck (Remember: I am facedown in a metal cocoon, so seeing any part of my body is difficult.), and reinserted the tube into my neck, once again delivering desperately-needed oxygen into my body. She then found staff and promptly told them what she thought of the care they were providing me. I am certain if she hadn't been there that day I would be dead right now.

Melinda never flinched at any of the diagnoses I was given. She stayed positive. After many weeks at the second hospital, they told my family and her that there was nothing else they could do for me. I had made it through all of the days and nights when I was expected to die, but my condition wasn't getting any better. Doctors gave me a zero percent chance of survival. A third hospital stepped in and said they would take me on as a patient, but they only gave me around a twenty percent chance to live. At the third hospital, they actually told her that I would lose my right arm and left leg, be mentally deficient, never be able to walk again, or would be a vegetable. She stuck around through all of that. She actually told staff, "I guess I'll have a goofy boyfriend to take care of then." I was dumbfounded when I was eventually told about how she had unwaveringly stuck by me through everything. So were the staff.

Every morning, Melinda would wake up around 5:00 a.m. She would shower in the tiny hospital room shower and drive forty-five minutes to her job. After completing a full day, she would then drive back to the hospital to be at my bedside. And this wasn't just after I woke up. She did this when I was unresponsive and they were telling her the worst.

After I did wake up, it was Melinda that fed me most of my meals. After going to work all day, she would stand at my bedside with a smile on her face and feed me dinner. She never showed that she was tired or worried. Whenever she was with me, she was smiling and had a positive attitude. After she fed me and I had my nightly treatments, we would watch TV. She held up through it all like a person for whom that was their only job. After everything she did for me during the day, she would go to sleep on a pull-out chair, exhausted, only to be woken up at least three times every night when staff checked on me. She never once complained.

Melinda also kept up with my chart and the care I was getting. On more than one occasion, she told staff that they were not doing their jobs correctly and made sure they took care of me properly. She learned the medical terms, how to read charts, the medications I was on and the proper dosages. If the staff were bandaging my wounds improperly she would correct them. She watched new staff members closely, and if they started to use the wrong ointment she would hand them the correct one. They were amazed by her knowledge, and many thought she was a physician. Melinda can be hard on herself and doesn't give herself credit for being very smart. I honestly do not know where she gets this; she is one of the smartest people I know. Who else could learn so much in such a short period of time? I sincerely don't know what I would have done without her. She is such a blessing from God.

Despite all of the demands on her time—working, learning about my condition, and caring for me—she unselfishly remained focused on my needs instead of her own. Emotionally, she was a rock. A day or so before I woke up, she was sitting by my bedside talking to me. She had made a decision that I don't know I could have made regarding a loved one. She decided to tell me it was okay if I wanted to go. As much as she wanted me to survive, if I could hear her while in my coma, she wanted me to know that it was okay if I stopped fighting. She leaned over my bed and whispered in my ear, "It's okay, baby. You've fought a good fight. It's okay if you go now. It's okay if it's too much to keep struggling to live. I love you and will be hurt so much, but if you need to go, you can go."

I cannot imagine saying the same thing to her. I am too selfish a person. I would want to keep holding on to the hope that she would pull through even if it meant she was uncomfortable or struggling. I can't imagine what it was like for her to do that, the suffering she must have seen me in to make that statement...I can only imagine. I'm sure the suffering she was enduring was much greater than anything I can ever come to terms with. She is the biggest blessing I have been given in my life; I love her.

[6]
TIME TO FIGHT

THE ABILITY TO TALK; the ability to feed myself; the ability to dress myself; the ability to stand; the ability to walk; the ability to go back to work in any meaningful capacity: these were all things that, when I woke up from my coma, I was told might not happen again. Why were they saying these things? Of course I would walk again. Why wouldn't I? There was not a doubt in my mind that I was going to walk again. Of course I would go back to work. How would I be *me* if I didn't work? I didn't understand the mentality of the hospital staff. What kind of patient would listen to this nonsense? *I* certainly wasn't listening to them. I shook off what they were telling me and decided it was time to get to work.

As all of the medication left my body and my mind grew clearer every day, the feeling of not being able to sit up without passing out or vomiting pissed me off. My body was weak, but my mind was coming back. I had been through some intensive training throughout my life, whether it be law enforcement-related, martial arts, or weightlifting. All had taught me to have a strong mind, and I would use that training during this process like I never had before.

I was given physical therapy (PT) in the hospital once a day for what seemed like ten minutes. The therapists who helped me were the greatest. They were positive but also worked to motivate me. They gave me the chance to succeed, while I felt others were holding me back by telling me to slow down or that something wasn't possible. At first, my PT consisted simply of sitting on the side of the bed attempting to support my own body weight. The first time I did this, I was too weak to control my legs or really any part of my body. To get me into position, they would raise the head of my bed as high as it would go. Another staff member would then grab my feet and start to slowly slide my legs off of the right side of the bed, turning my body until I was in an almost upright seated position. When I was ready, they would let go of my legs, letting them hang down to the ground, and would push my torso into an upright position. One person would be in front of me holding my wrists, while another would be behind me to support my upper body. I was like a newborn baby; I had no control of my body. I could hold the position for only a few seconds before I would start to dip sideways or, God forbid, forward. Staff would quickly grab me, toss my feet back up onto the bed, and let me lie back down. I would almost pass out from doing this small assisted movement, and afterwards, I would vomit. During these PT sessions, the staff had to make sure all of the tubes and lines hooked up to me didn't get caught on something or pulled loose. To me, though, there were only two important lines: the oxygen tube stuck up my nose and the catheter stuck up another area. Lord help me if this one got snagged and pulled at all! Every progression I made in movement, I made sure someone was dedicated to this line alone to make sure it had plenty of room to move freely! Even during our weakest and most "out of it" times, we still instinctively know where the most pain will come from and fear it.

We take for granted the muscles which control our most basic body positions and movements, such as sitting upright. I felt as if I literally had no muscles left in my body. Add to this the fact that I was lacking the equilibrium needed to keep from getting dizzy while being moved from a lying to a sitting position. It's a scary and strange feeling when you go from being an able-bodied person to one for whom even the act of sitting stationary and supporting your own body weight is the hardest exercise imaginable. Reality still hadn't sunk in yet. That would come later in rehabilitation. For now, I was frustrated with the general task at hand and focused on working to improve.

I considered every day a training day. Every chance I had, I tried to be independent. Most people don't realize how embarrassing it is to be unable to do the very basics for themselves. When people would visit me they would always tell me to go ahead and eat while they talked to me. I weighed less than two hundred pounds at this point and desperately needed to put on more weight to be strong enough for my eventual trip to the rehabilitation facility. I usually had a tray in front of me with some food and a drink on it. "Eat," I was told, but I never would. I didn't want them to see me looking like a cripple, trying my hardest just to grip a fork or spoon. I no longer had the dexterity to hold a utensil. I felt like a freak when I ate. My hands would shake, and I would drop food on myself because I didn't have the strength or coordination to put the food to my mouth. Half of the time, I would miss my mouth altogether. I would lean forward and try to meet the food halfway. When I did get it right, I took huge, awkward bites and then would almost choke on my food trying to make my jaw work. This was a big obstacle for me. I couldn't understand why chewing was so difficult. I couldn't manage to take appropriately-sized bites of food and get them down my throat, no matter how consciously I considered each bite or how small of a bite I took. I had seen handicapped people eating before and wondered why they looked the way they did when they ate, with part of the food coming out of their mouth and shoveling huge amounts of food in like they hadn't eaten in days. Now I was experiencing what I'm sure they go through during every meal: a feeling of being ashamed and not wanting people around while you are eating, a feeling of not being "normal." I realized I had to become aware of every movement I made now and work my hardest to get back to where I was before. I wasn't going to let this be my new normal. Every common action was a challenge now and had to be broken down into steps. This was the only way I could wrap my head around what was going on and formulate a plan to correct things.

One of my first challenges was to learn how to drink properly. I had been given the standard-issue huge plastic hospital cup with a lid and straw attached. It would be filled with shaved ice and water and placed on the tray that sat over my bed. I would shake so badly trying to pick this thing up...it felt like it weighed a hundred pounds! Once when I had visitors, I wanted a drink terribly, but I didn't want them to see how bad off I really was. As I talked to my friends by my bedside, I reached for the cup and struggled to lift it off the tray. As I fought to control it, the plastic cup started to shake from side to side, worsening as I brought it up and tried to get the straw into my mouth. While I tried to get the angle of the straw just right, my mouth would gape open for an extended period of time. When I finally got the straw in my mouth and started to drink, I looked up at my friends. They were looking at me with a bit of concern but mostly, as it seemed to me, with pity. I was shaking so badly I almost spilled half of the water on my lap. I was mortified. In my mind, I imagined what I thought they were thinking. They were looking at me like a poor cripple who couldn't do for himself, a poor cripple who couldn't even hold a cup to his mouth to take a drink of water. I was no cripple, and I certainly wasn't going to be looked at like one. I decided I would sit and talk to visitors until they left my room and only then eat and drink as quickly as possible. By this time, however, I was usually exhausted and quickly fell asleep.

Another activity I remember trying so hard to look normal while doing was talking on the phone. When I wanted food, I would call the kitchen on the hospital phone and place my order, and they would bring it to my room. I couldn't hold the phone to my ear and talk, nor could I prop the phone on my shoulder to keep my hands free. I was too weak for either method to work. I used a combination of the two and attempted to look as natural as possible in case anyone walked in the room. I remember when one of the custodial workers came in to clean my room when I was on the phone. He was a nice guy. He would tell me I was looking better every day and go about his job, but I also noticed he would watch me while he worked. It was a strange feeling. I felt like he was watching an animal in the zoo. I had tubes and probes coming out from everywhere. I had a ton of machines hooked up to me. I had scars on my neck, face, and head. I must have looked pretty interesting or even scary. But I remember trying so hard to look normal in front of him while I was on the phone. Was this what life was going to be like from now on—trying to fake looking normal? Waiting until I was alone to complete some simple task and then struggling to do so? I couldn't think about this too much. I wouldn't let myself get upset...not yet at least. I had too much work to do to start getting emotional at this point.

Breakfast was a scary and embarrassing time of day for me. By this time, I was using a remote attached to my bed to raise and lower the head of the bed myself. This was a workout in itself. The controller had some basic push buttons to control the bed movement, but I was so weak that even getting the buttons depressed enough to work took all the strength I had. After I got the bed into position, my breakfast would be placed on a sliding tray over my lap. Someone would return about an hour later to retrieve what was left. On the plate in front of me would be a container of juice with a sealed cover and a sealed straw. For most people this would be no obstacle at all. For me, though, it was an almost impossible barrier. There was no way I could get the straw out from the plastic package, so I quickly found that I could use the provided knife to slowly cut it open. I then tried to poke the straw through the seal over the juice, but this proved impossible. It might as well have well been sealed with steel. I had to take the knife and stab the top of the juice to make a hole I could put the straw through. After accomplishing this, I would shakily grab the juice and bring it to my lips to get a drink. By the time I made it to eating the actual breakfast, I was worn-out tired. I wouldn't ask for help, though. I had to learn to do this myself.

PT couldn't come quickly enough each day. It was only offered once a day, but after a couple of times, I requested an additional session. This probably wasn't the best idea, but I wanted to push myself. Sometimes they were able to give me an extra session, but many days, their list of patients was just too long and they could only come by once. Not a person to wait on help, I decided that if they couldn't make the extra session then I would do one myself. I couldn't stand by myself or even really sit up, but there were other things I could work on. In the mornings, I would sit upright using the electric bed and would place my hands facedown on the tray in front of me. I would try to lift my arms, both at the same time, as high as I could—almost like doing front raises at the gym but with no weights. I would do maybe three or four reps before dropping my hands like heavy lead weights back onto the tray. After a few sets, I would lie back in bed to keep from passing out. After a rest, when I felt like I had my faculties about me again, I would do another set. This process continued until I was too tired and would fall asleep sitting up against the bed.

My physical therapy progressed fairly quickly, from what I

was told. The therapists would time me every time I sat up, and each time, I would beat the previous day's number. I was on the sixth floor and was lucky enough to have a window on the right side of my room that looked down onto the parking garage. To help keep me from getting faint so quickly and to take my mind off the discomfort of being in a non-supported seated position, I was told to look outside and pick a spot to concentrate on. I could see the top of the parking garage and could clearly make out people getting out of their cars and walking down the stairs. This was my one glimpse into the world outside that was passing me by. I say discomfort because there wasn't pain, per se, but more a fear of fainting or losing my breath, even though I was still hooked up to oxygen. It made no sense to me why I felt so faint so quickly doing something that most people do for hours a day, but just sitting wore me out. Why I couldn't seem to catch my breath even though I was being given a large amount of continuous oxygen was also confusing. Nothing made sense anymore.

After several sessions of sitting on the side of the bed, the therapists asked me if I was ready to stand. I could barely sit upright without people holding onto me, but I wanted to stand. I wanted it more than anything at the time. They prepared me by putting me into my normal sitting position on the side of the bed. Then one of the staff members pulled out a piece of equipment that hadn't been used on me yet: they put an assistance belt around my waist. It was a canvas belt about four-inches wide and fifty-inches long with a slide-style buckle on the front for quick sizing. Years ago, I worked in a hospital for the mentally and physically disabled. I had used the same exact assistance belts, or gate belts, to grab onto the patients that could walk but were at a risk of falling. Basically, they give caretakers something to hold onto, either to give patients extra stability or to provide something to grab onto if they are about to tumble to the ground. Having the hospital staff put one of these around my waist immediately stirred up a wide range of emotions, making me sad, embarrassed, and pissed off. I told them to take it off of me, but it was mandatory. I think the anger helped me in this situation. Everything seemed to have come full circle. Years ago, I had been the one caring for a person like me, trying to help them in their struggles to move and be what I would consider more "normal." I hated it, but if I was going to stand and possibly walk again, I had to use the belt. As I sat on the side of the bed, someone stood in front of me holding my wrists while one staff member stood behind me holding onto the belt and two people on either side of me also held onto the belt. On the count of three, they pulled me into a standing position, and I pushed my heels into the ground with all I had. It happened quickly, and I was standing...finally standing. To keep from toppling over right away, I locked my knees. Of course, this was a bad thing to do, but it kept me up just long enough. I looked out onto the parking garage and the entire moving world outside. For the first time in months, I saw cars on the road, people walking, and trees. Oh, God—a literal window into the outside world! A look at what "normal" people were doing. And nature—the trees were wonderful. All of this was taken in in approximately three seconds. My legs quickly gave out, but the staff caught me before I fell and laid me back into bed. I began to cough and gasp for air. Phlegm was filling my throat and what felt like my lungs. I started to hyperventilate, and then I vomited. The staff quickly moved from therapy mode to caregiver mode, monitoring my stats. I was given a shot of pain medication that would also relax and knock me out. As I caught my breath and felt the pain medication kick in, I eased into a deep sleep, but that image of the outside world was burned into my mind. For the first time in what seemed like forever, I felt like I had earned my rest and had done something productive. Standing had also given me hope that I would walk again someday.

As the days went on and I settled into a routine, the knowledge of my condition hit me. Things had moved so quickly up until now that I hadn't had a chance to really evaluate what was going on, at least not to the point that it bothered me and truly sank in. Unless you've been through something physically traumatic and been isolated from the rest of the world for some time you can't know what I'm talking about. For the first time, I started to evaluate my situation: I wasn't normal anymore. I wasn't involved in the same world as everyone else. Time was passing me by. Everyone else's lives were going on, but I was stuck in this damn hospital bed. My friends were at work patrolling the city. My buddies were at the gym making progress and preparing for the next upcoming powerlifting meet. My girlfriend...my girlfriend was at work, eating lunch, visiting with family. She was having to get by on her own. She wasn't getting text messages from me every hour like she used to. She had no one to share her thoughts with, no one to share stories from her day with. Because of me, her day was consumed with worry and stress, and I was stuck in this bed just trying to stand. Never once did I doubt that Melinda would stay with me, but I didn't want this to be our new dynamic. I was supposed to be her protector. I was supposed to provide for her. How could I, though, if I couldn't even stand without help? If I wasn't motivated before, I certainly was now. I tried to be realistic about my healing and progression back to normal life, but I remember thinking, *How long will this last?* Would I be in a hospital like this for weeks, months, maybe even years, trying to get my independence back? Trying to just get back to normal, if that was even possible? Once again, anger set in. Tomorrow, I would stand twice as long. I had to get out of here. I had to heal my body. I had to get back out in the world. I had to get back to my job as a police officer, to lifting weights with my friends, but most importantly now, I had to get back to my role as a protector for Melinda.

The next day, I stood twice. The first time followed the same procedure: staff got me into position, counted to three, and hoisted me upright, and I got to see the wonderful outside world. This time, I think I stood for around five or six seconds before collapsing back onto the bed. As I caught my breath, I motioned to the PT staff, who were documenting my time and were about to leave. Although I could scarcely form the words, I asked if I could stand again. I waved my arms and held up two fingers as if to say, "Let me go a second time." They looked at me curiously and told me they normally didn't have anyone ask to go a second time. I had to, though. The anger was coming back, and I wanted to stand again! This was the same anger I used in the gym to get pumped up to do a heavy lift. This was the same motivation I used when I was at work and knew I was going into a violent situation. I used this to get myself prepared for what was becoming my new challenge, and it was going to be one hell of a fight!

After a brief rest, I was repositioned on the side of the bed, and the count began. I psyched myself up mentally. I pictured myself going for a max lift in the gym. I was going to fight with a violent criminal. I was going to stand up for Melinda. One big effort was all...one more time. When I heard the word "three" from the therapist, I forced my damaged heels into the floor and strained with all my might. Not much happened on my end, but the staff did their job and got me to a standing position. This time, I stayed up for an additional six seconds. I was shaking, and I'm sure I had the most pissed-off look on my face, straining to stay up, straining to not pass out. I collapsed back down again, exhausted. I started laughing this time, and again, the staff looked at me like I was crazy. They didn't understand—I was so happy! I had just stood up twice and for longer than I had the previous time. I was overjoyed! Nothing could have made me happier that day, but that wasn't going to be enough. I wanted to walk before I left for rehab, and I wanted to get off of the catheter. I'm not sure which was harder. That's not true. Walking, or my version of walking, was much easier.

I continued, every day, to make progress, sometimes standing for almost twenty seconds and without that damn gate belt for assistance! When I did finally take my first steps, they weren't forward nor did they involve picking my feet up off the ground. My first "steps" consisted of shuffling my feet to the right and then trying to shuffle them back to the left. And when I say shuffled, I mean that I shifted my right foot maybe a couple of inches on the floor and then shifted it back. Then I would do the left foot. "Congratulations, you just walked two steps!" As lame as it sounds, they gave me credit for the steps, and I got high fives all around. By the time I was done, I was taking two or three small steps forward to an awaiting recliner that I would sit up in for as long as I possibly could before leaning it back. The ability to stay upright without feeling like I was going to pass out remained an issue well into rehab and actually for some time after I went back home. I'm not sure when this actually started to dissipate, but it was one of the more difficult things to overcome.

One day, my parents came to visit me, and when they walked into the room, my bed was empty. I was only a few feet away, but to see me sitting up in a chair shocked them. I was so proud of myself. I felt almost normal again. It was strange to look at the bed where I had lain for some three plus months. Finally being away from it almost brought tears to my eyes. At last, I was making what I considered real progress!

One more task had to be completed, however, before I could transfer to rehab. Having to hit a button to ask a grown man or woman to bring in a bedpan and try to lift my body up and slide the pan under my butt was awkward, to say the least. But trying to use the restroom lying flat as a board with a pan—hopefully, centered—under my butt was about as bad as it gets. (Well, not quite as bad as it gets, but I'll get to that shortly.) Now that I was able to stand and pivot to the recliner with assistance, it was finally time to try to stand and pivot to a portable toilet (basically, a toilet lid on a chair built out of PVC tubing with a trash bag underneath it). Now, you have to understand: at this point, things were critical to me. My catheter had previously been removed, only to have to be reinserted. If you're a guy, this is something you only want to experience when you are unconscious like I was the first time. The second time it was inserted was after I failed to stay conscious while using the upright portable toilet. If you've never had a catheter put in, the pain is about as bad as you are guessing it to be, so I was *highly* motivated to make it work this second time. Remember: I was still getting faint when standing or seated upright. Yet I would have to stand, get cleaned, *and* pivot again back to the bed. To possibly understand, put yourself in the position of a person who is physically handicapped. Everything a handicapped person does physically is measured beforehand. How many steps will this task take? How many seconds will I have to remain upright? What is the plan if I get stuck in between any part of the movement? This particular movement had many areas of concern for me, but I had to complete it this time. I'm not sure how close I came to passing out while trying, but I know I finally succeeded on the second try and collapsed into bed. It is all a blur, but I know I hit the bed laughing. Now even the regular staff was looking at me strangely. I couldn't help it. I was so happy! While I lay in bed, they called two of my work buddies who were driving in from training and had me on speakerphone. I was so happy about what I had just done that I blurted out, "I just took a shit! I just took a shit on a normal toilet!" I couldn't contain myself. They burst out laughing. Between trying not to crash and laughing so loud I had to pull the phone away from my ear, they congratulated me on the "great accomplishment." It was an amazing ending to the day.

ANOTHER DANCE WITH DEATH

I WAS awake to experience my fourth brush with death, which still haunts me and causes me to have nightmares to this day. When the speaking device was inserted in my neck I was pointedly instructed that I could not sleep with it on. The device had a thin piece of paper in the middle that could get clogged very easily, and since it was placed in my airway, if it were to become clogged I could easily suffocate and die. Just to drive the point home, I was told a cautionary tale about a woman who was released from this same hospital to a rehab facility with one of these speaking devices still in place. The staff at this facility were not well versed on the device, and she fell asleep with hers in. Phlegm built up in the paper of the device, and she died...suffocated. The rehab staff found her dead when they were doing their normal rounds. This scared me but did not save me from almost coming to the same end. The night before the incident, the nurse on duty showed me how to call for help if I lost my alarm remote, which I had in the bed with me at all times. It was a remote attached to the end of a cord that was draped over the side of the bed. Everyone knows how easy it is to lose a television remote in bed. With the number of sheets I had on my bed at the time and not being able to stand up and toss the sheets if something was lost, items could be misplaced very easily. The nurse on shift that evening told me that if I had an emergency and could not find the remote to rip the leads off of my chest, and a monitor would show a flat line to nurses in the hallway who would come and help me. Now that my condition had improved a bit, I didn't have constant supervision like I did in the beginning of my stay at the hospital. Sometimes staff would be out of the room for an hour or so at a time. This particular morning, I had woken up, eaten breakfast, and was watching television in bed, waiting for my PT session. My speaking device had been put in after I had eaten. I began to get tired and thought it would be a good idea to rest my eyes before my workout. I had gotten comfortable enough with the device that I had become lax. I laid my head back, thinking I would just close my eyes for a second, but before I knew it, I had begun to drift off to sleep. Things seemed to happen in an instant. There was no coughing, then wheezing, then gasping for breath. Seemingly in an instant, I couldn't breathe! I struggled to sit up in bed like anyone's instinct would have him do but did not have the strength. I had the natural instinct everyone has when choking to stand up and bend over in an attempt to either get better airflow or to clear the blockage from my throat, but I didn't have the ability to do either of these actions. I couldn't even cough to clear my throat yet. Imagine holding your breath while sitting still and not trying to fight to breathe until every bit of air was already gone from your lungs. That's what I was going through. I had zero air and no ability to help myself.

I desperately grabbed for my emergency remote to alert the staff, but I couldn't find it. As I struggled to get a breath, I ran my hand through every layer of the sheets, but I still couldn't find the remote. I was starting to see spots in my vision. I had to do something, or I knew I would die like the woman I had heard about. I was becoming dizzy. I struggled more and more to find the remote. Thinking I was about to pass out, I ripped at my hospital gown and, luckily, was able to move it off my chest. I felt desperately for the probes and, fortunately, grabbed a handful on the first try. I pulled as hard as I could, hoping I had the strength. I pulled and pulled and finally felt a release of pressure when I managed to pull one of the leads off. I grasped again and got hold of more. I pulled with all my might, and another lead came loose. When a patient hits the emergency button a nurse from the station down the hall would use the intercom system to call the room to make sure there was an actual emergency. *Lord, can't they see by their machines I am dying? Can't they tell I'm not breathing?* A nurse's voice came over the intercom, announced my room number, and asked if there was an emergency. I gasped, trying to speak, but nothing would come out. I was straining with everything I had to make a sound. *Please, Lord, let someone walk in the room now.* She called again, asking if there was an emergency. *Lord, don't let her think it was an accident. Please don't let her take her time coming to check on me!* I was scared and still couldn't breathe. My life didn't flash before my eyes like people say. My mind was too concerned with fighting and gasping for every bit of breath I could gather, but nothing was happening. I still couldn't get air! As I started to fade out, finally I saw nurses entering my room. They were talking to each other and seemed to be walking so slowly. I was panicked and waving my arms, motioning that I couldn't breathe! I was told to "calm down" and "just relax." One of them told me I was having a panic attack. I thought I saw the staff laughing while checking my vitals on the machines. *They don't get it,* I thought. *I'm going to die because these idiots don't get what's happening!* How could they be so relaxed about what was happening? I thank God that one of the respiratory therapists walked in, ran to my bedside, and ripped the speaking valve from my neck. Air immediately rushed in; I could breathe again! My vision had narrowed to a pinprick view but was now coming back into focus. I was scared beyond belief. The nurses watched me for a bit and still told me that I just needed to calm down. I was too worn out to be angry at this point. Then the situation got worse. One nurse looked at my side and realized that I had messed myself. She wasn't happy. It was everywhere. They had to change my sheets, clean up a huge mess, and re-dress me. I'm sure it wasn't the most pleasant thing to have to do, but I didn't do it intentionally. While getting me cleaned up, they placed me in a padded rolling chair. I'm not sure why they did this. After what I had just been through, most conscientious people would realize that I might be tired and need to rest. The staff that were with me on this day, though, had a different idea. I will never say anything against the hospital in general, but every place has employees that shouldn't be doing the jobs they are doing. These employees were just those people. What I did wasn't on purpose, but it seemed like I was put in that chair as punishment. I was told by one female staff member who was standing behind me while they propped me up in the chair that I needed to "man up." *Really?* I thought...*man up?* Is that really what you should be saying to someone who almost just suffocated because you didn't have the job knowledge to solve the problem by pulling out his speaking device? I wasn't mad, though, at this point—I was scared. I was at these people's mercy. I was handicapped and needed everyone's assistance to make it through each day. I would die otherwise.

The chair they had placed me in was one that PT used to gradually train me to sit up straight without becoming dizzy. It was a very hard-backed and upright chair that you were strapped into with a seatbelt for safety so you wouldn't slink down and slide off the edge of the seat. Twice, staff had tried to put me in this chair, but the pain was so intense they never used it again.

Earlier, when I said I had a bedsore on my back that was down to the bone, I wasn't being one-hundred percent honest: it was actually on my tailbone—an embarrassing place to have such a wound but even more painful when you are forced to sit on it. The nursing staff placed me on this chair and gave me a sponge bath. The water was freezing cold, and they were rough with me. I remember being in pain, miserably cold, and scared. Where was Melinda? *Oh, God, I wish she were here to help me.* I tried to cry out in pain, but I no longer had my valve in and was again mute. After they were done wiping me down, they placed a hospital gown over the front of me and left me in the chair. I tried to tell them I wasn't supposed to stay in the chair, but they couldn't hear me nor did they see me mouthing to them. Left alone in my room, I wondered how long they were going to leave me in that chair. Thank God they left the door to my room open, though. I waved my arm to anyone that walked by, but I was so weak it barely moved, and no one ever really looked in at me anyway. All I could do was wave my arm and watch the clock on the wall in front of me. After being in the chair for a little over an hour, the president of the hospital came in. I was so happy to see him! Due to my unique case and my profession, he was kind enough to stop by and check on my status fairly regularly. I was so happy to see him I couldn't contain myself! Finally, someone who would help me! I mouthed the word "help" to him over and over. I tried to tell him I was in pain. I kept mouthing "pain, pain, pain," but he couldn't understand me. He shrugged his shoulders and said that he wasn't good at reading lips. I was so thankful he didn't just leave me but went and got someone who could help understand what I was mouthing to him. When he came back into my room with a familiar staff member whom I knew to be very helpful and kind I was overjoyed. She immediately saw the pain in my face and knew that I wasn't supposed to be in that chair due to the open wound on my tailbone. She quickly gathered other staff and moved me back to my bed. She also had someone bring me a new speaking valve. I quietly told them what had happened; they were appalled! I was uneasy about how the negligent nurses might react if I got them in trouble. They were supposed to keep me safe, but I was no longer able to trust them. It's a strange thing when you become dependent on people. I never understood why people would protect those who abused them and were scared to stand up for themselves. Now, I felt like a pathetic victim—something I never thought I would be. I cried and felt ashamed. I was quickly reassured that I had done nothing wrong and that the employees involved in this incident would no longer be allowed in my room. I was grateful.

I recalled from my years on patrol as a police officer that, at almost all the deaths I responded to, the deceased had apparently messed themselves. When the body is fighting to stay alive, it shuts down all non-essential functions, one of these being the bowels. I've seen many horrible things that come along with my job: I have seen people die in front of me, car accidents where body parts were strewn around in pieces more times than I can count, and I have been handed a dying baby by parents looking to me to save their child. At times, all of these memories give me nightmares, but the nightmare I have most often these days is from this event.

The majority of the staff I dealt with during this sickness were good people doing their best to take care of me. However, like in any line of work, there were some that shouldn't have been in the positions they were in. For instance, in law enforcement if you have someone who shouldn't be doing the job it isn't just going to cost the company some money or screw up a customer's order. It could mean life or death. The direct healthcare system is no different. There were a few others that I had to report to a supervisor, and those people never cared for me again; it was always handled. In one instance, a nurse decided my chart was too thick to read, so he was going to just "wing it" with my wound care. Thankfully, Melinda was present and made sure the situation was handled. On another occasion, when I asked for assistance to stand up and urinate into the portable bedside toilet, the caregiver sounded put out and asked me why I couldn't just urinate into a cup while lying down so he didn't have to help me get out of bed. Both of these "care providers" were lazy, and both were dealt with. If you are a patient or a patient's family member, know that if you feel like something is not being handled correctly, you have the right to request that a particular employee (or employees) no longer be allowed to provide care for you or your loved one. It's imperative to their safety and the safety of others who might have to receive "care" from them in the future.

My time in this facility was coming to a close. I was progressing quickly, and my doctors wanted to get me into a rehabilitation facility. I was glad to hear this even though I still had many issues. Practically every day, it seemed like another tube was being removed from my body. With each tube that was removed I felt a bit freer. I remember when they pulled the pic line out of my left arm. It was a long tube stuck down into my arm to administer medicine directly into my bloodstream without having to continually stick me with a needle. I'm not sure exactly how long it was, but it seemed as though it was ten inches long. I felt no pain, but Melinda almost passed out. I also remember when they pulled the tubes out of the side of my chest. I had four tubes on my right side, and they were large as well—more so in diameter, though. They looked like giant drinking straws. I felt no pain during this process either. I was just glad to have them out. A short time later, I was finally ready to be transported to the rehabilitation facility.

I remember the day of the transport: I was excited beyond belief! I was warned that rehab would be the hardest part of my recovery and that only a small part of the challenge would be physical. The bigger hurdle would be mental. I didn't listen to them. I had been through some tough experiences and felt like I could handle this next one as well. How hard could it be? I had endured some difficult training at work. I had been through some crazy training while studying martial arts, as well as some tough experiences in the gym. Nothing, however, had prepared me for this next challenge. Mentally, it broke me.

[8]
MY DAILY MANTRA

I WILL CONQUER *what's not been conquered.*

Defeat will not be in my creed.

I will believe what others have doubted.

I have trained my mind, and my body will follow.

I will acknowledge the fact that my opponent does not expect me to win, but I will never surrender.

Weakness will not be in my heart.

I will look to my comrades and those who have brought me into this world and those who have trained me, and I will draw strength from them.

I will gladly go off into the field of battle; and I will move, groove, and do everything I can do; and I will reach my field of battle by any means at my disposal; and when I get there, I will arrive violently.

I will rip the heart from my enemy and leave it bleeding on the ground, 'cause he cannot stop me.

No one will deny me. No one will define me. And no one will tell me who and what I am and can be.

Belief will change my world.

It has moved continents; it has moved countries and has put man on the moon, and it will carry me through this battle.

Defeat, retreat: those are not my words. I don't understand those definitions.

I don't understand when things go wrong.

I don't understand mistakes, but I do understand this: I understand victory, and I understand never surrendering.

No matter how bad things go, my heart and my mind will carry my body when my limbs are too weak.

Today will be that day. Not tomorrow. Not next week but right now, right here in your house and in your home.

History will remember me. I will not have to worry about him being kind.

I will define myself. I will right my own praises, and no one will tell me what I can and cannot be.

And I will never go home, not without giving everything I have got.

————

There is a reason many people spend long periods of time in rehab. There is also a good reason many relationships last throughout the hospitalization period but end when the patient goes into rehab. I'm not sure if rehab was considered so tough because of the demanding environment or if it is so mentally taxing because you finally see what your limitations are based on your condition and have to face them head on. I was told I would be in rehab for six months to a year. I was also told I would be in a wheelchair for much of that time. But I was out of rehab in less than three weeks, and I walked out.

After an entire day of getting settled into the rehab facility, I began my therapy right away. I started off with two physical therapy (PT) sessions and one occupational therapy (OT) session a day. The days started early—around 6:00 a.m. Breakfast would be served, and then three days a week, an assistant would help me get cleaned up for the day. The first time I was asked about taking a shower I lied and said I had already had one. I recalled how cold and miserable sponge baths had been at the previous hospital. I required total assistance at this time, which made me feel both scared and embarrassed. Both of my feet were still bandaged, as well as my lower back. I was also still too weak to really stand, and my motor skills were very poor, so doing things like getting dressed or drying myself with a towel were next to impossible.

When I was finally forced to take a shower my wounds had to be covered to make sure the bandages didn't get wet. Basically, I had two trash bags on my feet, taped at the top in an attempt to water-proof them, and one flattened bag taped over my butt. I was then wheeled into the en suite bathroom. I was connected to oxygen from a wall-mounted unit beside my bed via about fifty feet of tubing that I had to manipulate, which made things difficult to maneuver around the room, but I managed. After being wheeled into the bathroom and getting undressed while in the wheelchair, I would receive assistance standing and pivoting onto a shower chair in the open shower. The shower didn't have a door or a lip to step over. It was simply a shower head with a curtain around it to keep the water from splashing everywhere while the patient was showering. I got into position on the chair and was handed the shower head. I can't describe how amazing the feeling of hot water running over me was, but it seemed as great as when I took my first drink of water after waking up. I held the shower head over my head and almost cried. I hadn't had a hot shower in months. Of course, I realize I wasn't conscious for a lot of this time, but the portion for which I had been awake felt like months by itself. When put in a situation where you are taken completely out of your normal routine, even a week can feel like an eternity. I had probably been conscious for a month by now, and that was long enough. I probably didn't get very clean during this first shower. I had so much trouble trying to use the soap, but I did the best I could. Mostly, I held the shower head over my head as long as I could and then let it rest on my leg and hit me in the chest. After sitting there for as long as I could, I was told I had to get out. I required assistance drying off and getting dressed. Because of my thickly bandaged and swollen heels, I wasn't able to wear shoes yet.

While in the bathroom, I purposefully avoided looking in the mirror. There had been no opportunity to look in a mirror at the previous hospital because I was stuck in bed, not able to make it to the actual bathroom. I had asked for a mirror when I first woke up, but my family and caregivers thought it best for me not to see myself because of how I looked at the time. They didn't want me to get upset. I had sustained damage to the tip of my nose from a mask I had to wear while in the RotoProne bed that had cut into my face. I almost lost my nose entirely, but luckily, it was caught before it got that bad. I also had scars on the right side of my face and neck, one across my forehead, on my chest, under my pec, and on my side; and I was missing hair on the right side of my head. I would have to look eventually...just not yet.

After getting dressed for the day, I was wheeled to the therapy room where I would begin my therapy sessions. I was wheeled up to a table and given putty and a piece of paper with a bunch of shapes drawn on it. I was told to form the putty into the shapes shown on the paper and to complete each one until I couldn't go any further down the list. I went through the whole list, first with one hand and then with the other. It was tough, but I used my palm and the side of my hand to help shape and compress the putty into the proper forms. The therapist assigned to me didn't quite seem to believe that I had worked through all of the shapes with both hands. I was happy with my progress on general dexterity. When I first woke up from my coma, a good friend from the gym brought me a pen and a journal. He got this for me to practice my handwriting and to document my thoughts about what was happening. It was a great gesture on his part. When he presented it to me, I took the pen and tried to write the current date at the top of the first page. This was an almost impossible feat. My hand was shaking so badly that I had a lot of trouble just trying to grip the pen. I did my best, and my friend was nice enough to write the actual date beside my attempt. One month later, I wrote the current date again, and my handwriting was already back.

Sometimes when you are told you can't do something you really *can't* do it. Other times, you really can, but most people won't put in the effort to make it possible. I believe in putting in the effort to make it possible. I have faith in myself and faith in God to help me. But I don't believe God will help those who refuse to first help themselves. I never once asked for God to save me. I only asked for God to help me best deal with the situation at hand. It is up to me to put forth the effort and work and try until I can no longer try anymore. Then, I must get up and try again. I prayed a lot when I was in the hospital. I prayed to thank God for saving me, not to get me out of the situation or to recover faster. I prayed with friends and family, and every time, it was the same—giving thanks for God being so great. Now my prayers were different. Now I prayed for strength to carry me through this physical and mental battle.

This chapter opened with part of a speech I heard years ago given by a football coach trying to motivate his decidedly underdog team. I changed some of the speech to better fit my situation. I have used it at work many times when I felt like I wasn't mentally prepared for a dangerous situation I was about to go into. I also used it before powerlifting meets to get my thought process right for competition. Now I use it when I have hard days

I'm not sure I can make it through. I used it in rehab many times. The mind is a powerful thing, and getting in the right frame of mind during a difficult time like I was going through might be the difference between failure and success.

My main goal in rehab was to walk again. I would wheel myself to the PT room where I would be given a walker with an attached seat and basket. After locking the wheels on my wheelchair, I would lift myself into a standing position and grab the handles of the walker. I would then unlock the walker's wheels using the hand brakes while a staff member unlocked the wheels on the wheelchair. Walking forward, I would see how many steps I could take, while the staff member followed behind with the wheelchair. The first time, I think I walked about five steps before falling back into the wheelchair. Again, I would get up and try to walk another five steps. I continued this until I couldn't go any further. I was constantly on supplemental oxygen, and the air pressure would be raised and lowered depending on what my levels were. They also tested to see how long it took me to recover from each attempt at walking. Like any workout, the main exercise (walking) was followed by assistant exercises to help strengthen the muscles. Sometimes I would do lower body and sometimes I would do upper body exercises. After these sessions, I was wheeled back to my room to await lunch and to rest up for my second PT session of the day. During these breaks, I enjoyed sitting in my wheelchair and looking out the window. I didn't get much downtime to simply sit and look outside, and seeing trees again was relaxing. This facility was a one-story building, and my room's window faced an open field with trees. Off to the left, I could see a bit of road with cars going by, which was both a blessing and a curse. It was great to see normal activities again like people going to and from work or running errands, but it was mentally draining to see people doing what I no longer could. When I would see squad cars going by, I would wonder which buddy of mine might be working and what call he or she was going to—not that I knew anymore what shifts people were working. I had completely lost track of time. Things that had been second nature to me—what day it was or who was working what shift—were now just meshed together.

During my second PT session of the day, I did a lot of assistance work: exercises like leg and arm raises that would improve my strength for the main therapy in the morning. Sometimes the program would change, but this was the main routine I followed. One exercise that was truly sobering for me was the front arm raise with dumbbells. Most of the time, I was seated in my wheelchair next to a very old woman. She used a pair of blue dumbbells for front raises and curls. These were the rubber-coated, color-coded dumbbells that I always thought were funny for some gyms to carry. Who would be so weak that they would have to use these? How embarrassing! As I sat watching and waiting for my next exercise, I spotted my helper walking toward me with something pink in her hands. As she got closer, I saw exactly what she was carrying. It was a pair of pink dumbbells, and they were for me. The blue ones that the woman beside me was using were around five pounds; these were even lighter—probably around two and a half pounds. She handed them to me and instructed me to perform ten front raises and ten curls. I think I got to around three front raises and gave out. I had to cheat and swing the rest to get them up. My curls were just about as pathetic. I could hardly believe what I used to use for these exercises in the gym. That all seemed so foreign to me now. Things that had seemed so easy now seemed impossible.

As I struggled through my PT and OT sessions, two things remained a constant source of motivation and got me through each day: my relationship with God and my girlfriend (now wife), Melinda. A few times a week, a pastor came to my room and asked if I wanted to pray. I would ask him to pray for two things: I wanted a good relationship with my parents and I wanted comfort and help mentally dealing with my struggles. I always felt better after I prayed. I felt truly close to God at this time. I think most people don't know what it is to really have a relationship with God. Put in the position I was, I was no longer burdened by material things or the distractions that other people had. None of that was important anymore. I believe I was witness to true evil like I had never felt before when I was in a coma, but I also felt that I had God and his angels fighting for me as well, fighting for my soul. I got a taste of both heaven and hell and received a glimpse of my future if I didn't choose the right path. I made the choice to fight, and God stood by me and gave me the power to live again. Now he was by my side every day of my rehab. I believe he has always been by my side, but now I could truly feel him with me.

I also had to believe that the things happening to me were for a reason. I certainly don't consider myself a *bad* person, but I think these struggles were a wake-up call from God. I could have been making better choices in my life, but I also think it was a wake-up call for people around me. Even though it was a relatively brief period of time, people told me that my illness and struggle had a profound effect on their lives. For some, it was simply learning to consciously treat every day as special, because you never know when it may be your last. For others, however, it meant a definitive change in their lives. One good friend of mine finally faced some major demons of his own and completely changed his life. Drug use and adultery were commonplace for him, but he finally had his eyes opened after I got sick. He quit all of the negative things his world revolved around. It cost him his marriage and probably some close friends, but he took a stance and did the right thing, and today he is a different person. He is clear-eyed, clear-headed, and has a clear conscience. That one person whose life was touched by me getting sick has made everything worth the struggle. Thinking about him and how other people might be gaining strength from my illness, as odd as it might seem, gave me strength to get through those days in rehab. It gave me motivation when I felt like quitting. How would quitting look to the people who were turning their lives around? I had to keep going.

Melinda continued her routine of staying with me every night like she had when I was in the hospital. She slept on a pull-out chair next to me. How uncomfortable it must have been for her to work a full shift at the vet clinic, drive to the rehab center, sit in a chair every afternoon beside me, and then sleep in the same chair, only to repeat the process every day for almost three weeks. And to think: she had done this for months already at the hospital. I loved her so much. She had shown such great loyalty and unconditional love.

I never liked anyone being present during my PT sessions, but one day when she got off work early, Melinda asked if she could watch. During this session, she got to witness me walk for the first time. Until then, I had kept people out of my room and away from me during PT because I was embarrassed. I was nervous, but excited to show her my progress. She was so supportive of me and always told me I was doing great and kissed me. She didn't care if I looked horrible and was sickly or smelled. The look in her eyes and on her face was the same one she had when we first started dating. This helped me push during these PT sessions. I wanted to show her that I was trying as hard as she was. I wanted to make her proud of me again. My steps were still being counted, but now my goal was to get to a fixed point. I wanted to show her how far I could walk. My first goal was to make it out into the hall. My next goal was to make it out into the hall *and* walk back in one try. Every day that I walked, I doubled what I had done the previous time. And every time I walked, I tried to look more "normal." A person's gait is a funny thing, something you don't think about much until yours looks strange. Regulating your gait is a difficult task when you have giant holes on your heels, huge bandages on your feet, and you're wearing flip-flops. The flip-flops were a great gift from Melinda, who had purchased new clothes to fit my smaller body. The staff had recommended that she purchase shoes one size bigger than normal to accommodate the bandages, but since I normally wore a size 14, that was difficult to do. The shirts she brought me stayed the same, though: mainly weightlifting-themed t-shirts—anything to keep me motivated.

———

Before I got sick, Melinda and I were sitting on the couch watching TV and looking on the Internet on my laptop. We were talking about what each of us wanted in our future and what it would take for us to marry someone. She told me that she had a dream purse she had always wanted and a dream ring. "If someone got me those things I would finally consider getting married." Of course, she was mostly joking, but I knew those were special things that no one else had gotten for her. So those two items became special to me. I bookmarked the website where the ring was found and memorized which purse she wanted (at least, I thought I did). One day when we were out shopping, we went by the store with the ring just so she could show it to me in person. I told her the ring looked nice, but the price was way too expensive. Along with the two matching bands, how could anyone afford that? She agreed it was really too much. We went by other stores and found cheaper rings that she liked, and I wrote down the information on them to show her I was keeping track. We talked about it a few more times and then stopped discussing it. It was just too much money for us at the time.

Christmas was coming around, and we were trying to save

money. We had just purchased a house. It was brand new and in a nice, quiet neighborhood just north of where we both worked. We had agreed that, this Christmas, we would only buy each other small presents and just enjoy the house. Melinda had done a great job decorating the house, too. She purchased the biggest Christmas tree I had ever seen! I had to buy a special ladder just to put the angel on top. I would sit and watch the reflection of the lights dancing on the windows behind the tree. She spent so much time making it perfect because she wanted our first Christmas together in the new house to be special.

A tradition in her family was for everyone to gather at a chosen family member's house and celebrate Christmas as a family, even if it wasn't on Christmas day. We had about an hour-long drive to get to the celebration, so we loaded up in the truck and were about to back out of the driveway when I told her that I thought I had accidentally left the water running in the master bedroom. How dumb of me... I asked Melinda to run back inside and make sure the water was off, just in case, so we didn't come home to a flooded bathroom. She looked at me a bit strangely then went back inside. A few minutes later, she came back outside, stopped in the front yard by the truck, and just stared at me. A few weeks before, I had sent a message to her sister to make sure I remembered the right purse that Melinda wanted—her dream purse. Her sister devised a plan to get the information from Melinda without alerting her and then texted me with the information. I ordered the purse and had it sent to the house. I planned to make sure I was there to get the package so she wouldn't accidentally get it off the porch and open it, ruining the surprise. The day it was set to arrive, I was waiting at the house all morning on my day off from work. The package was supposed to arrive no later than noon. Well, noon came and went and no package. I called the company, desperately looking for answers. This could ruin everything! I had ordered it in plenty of time for it to arrive a few days before Christmas. The customer service representative informed me the package had been lost, and it might be a few days before I got it. What came out of my mouth probably weren't the nicest sounding words, but the message got across because the rep said she felt bad and would do everything she could to make the situation right. Not holding out much hope, I started devising a plan B. The very next day, the woman from the company called me personally and told me the package would be arriving at the house in thirty minutes. It was a signature-only package, and I was at least forty-five minutes away. I raced home, cursing traffic and every traffic light I managed to hit. I just knew I would pull up and see a note on the door that I had missed the driver. But just as I pulled up so did the delivery truck. Melinda was still at work, so I had time to open the box. The purse was as it was supposed to be and came complete with its own special gift box and card.

That evening, before leaving for Melinda's family gathering, I removed the delivery box from its hiding spot in the closet, placed the purse inside its gift box with the card on top, and left it on the bathroom counter. As I walked out, I turned the faucet on so that when she walked into the bedroom she would hear the water running and find her surprise. Melinda was so happy and surprised when she got back into the truck with her purse! It made me feel so good to be able to do something for her that made her feel that special. Melinda isn't into material things. She couldn't care less if she wore the same shoes for two years or if she had an old cell phone. She had a few things, though, that were special to her, which she had been waiting for a man to give her to show that he cared and he was listening. I was happy to do that for her, no matter what the price.

———

During my next PT session, not only was Melinda there but also my sister Christina. This was a surprise. Normally, my sister would visit later in the afternoon and bring me a Route 44® Cherry Dr. Pepper® from a local fast-food restaurant. I love those and attribute part of my recovery to having at least two a week, thanks to my sister. This day, though, she was early. I had just finished practicing my walking when I saw them both watching along the far wall. I was resting in my wheelchair by a set of stairs with a railing, another training device. While I rested, an elderly woman went up and down the stairs doing her physical therapy. There were four steps up to a landing and four stairs going down. After a short rest, I was wheeled up to the stairs behind the older woman. Today would be my first attempt at stepping up onto anything. The woman walked up to the landing and back down with ease, then sat in her wheelchair. After she was wheeled off to the side, I was moved in front of the stairs. I was told to go up one stair and rest. I had not walked up anything at this point—not even a curb. Hell, I hadn't been outside to have the *chance* to walk up a curb. I did my one stair and sat down to rest. It was shaky, at best, but I was happy I was even able to get up it. I wanted to go again and was told this was fine but I had to rest first. As I waited, I looked over and saw Melinda and Christina watching me. They smiled and gave me thumbs up. But looking at the old woman who had gone before me, I started to get mad. To think: this old woman was going to show me up in front of my family. Forget that! I told staff I was ready to go again. I stood up from my wheelchair and grabbed onto the metal rail with my left hand. A therapist took hold of my oxygen line and grabbed onto my right arm for support, just in case I took a spill. I went up one stair and then another. I kept going until I got to the top. I wasn't able to turn around to come back down, so I just backed down slowly. When I got back to the bottom, I quickly fell into my wheelchair and began to gasp for breath. After turning up the oxygen level on my portable tank, the staff asked me what the heck I was thinking, doing that. I looked at the old woman and told them that I wasn't going to be shown up by a crippled old lady in front of my family. The old woman smiled at me; the staff shook their heads. Although I was mostly joking with the female patient (we talked occasionally during PT and knew each other.), in a way, I wasn't. I was tired of being in a rehab center with old people outperforming me. It had only been a couple of weeks, but it might as well have been a year. It was kind of sad, I guess, but each day after that, I would pick a person in the physical therapy room and try to beat them at an exercise. That was the only method I knew to make progress. I had to continue to push myself. This would prove to be another turning point for me.

My next occupational therapy session would be yet another turning point for me. I needed to learn how to dress myself without any assistance. Because I had major mobility issues making it difficult to raise my arms above my head or to bend down to put socks on, the staff helped me put on most of my clothes. To overcome this challenge, I was given two wooden rods with a kind of hook on the back. They were assistance devices for handicapped people to allow them to be more independent. Immediately, I recalled them from my time working at the state school years ago. They were the same devices used to help those permanently disabled men get dressed. I remembered how old and dirty those assistance devices always looked. Why couldn't they make them out of aluminum or something nicer-looking that could be kept clean? A lot of the equipment those guys used always looked old and depressing, and now here I was being handed the same tool. As instructed, I practiced using the device to put my shirt and socks on during this session in the physical therapy room.

I was ashamed. I was probably one of the patients in the worst shape at this facility, and I would catch the other patients watching me, probably wondering why a young guy like me had the major issues I did and wondering what had happened to me.

Left alone later in my room, I looked out the window and cried. I couldn't believe this was who I had become: a damn cripple in a wheelchair who couldn't even walk without assistance and who had to use old, dirty-looking wooden rods to get himself dressed! I hid the devices in the closet next to my bed so Melinda wouldn't ask me about them. But getting ready for my morning PT session the next day, I used the devices to get dressed. I was able to get my shirt over my head and put on my socks by myself. This would be the last time I would use them. I put them back in the closet and went to my PT session. When I got back, I showered by myself for the first time. When I wheeled myself into the bathroom, I also looked in a mirror for the first time since my coma. I was in my wheelchair in just a pair of shorts. At first, I didn't recognize myself. I knew I had lost weight, but I never imagined I would look like this. I thought I would just look like I did when I was younger and thinner. That's not how it worked, though. Almost every bit of muscle I had on my body was gone, including the muscles in my face, which made a huge impact on my appearance. I looked like what I was: a sick man who was fighting off death, someone who needed around-the-clock assistance and could not take care of himself. I was pale, and my hair was thin and wispy. I made a point to keep it shaved, yet it was still so sparse and patchy. I had a large bald spot on the right side of my head where tubes had rubbed against me when I was on ECMO. I also had a dark line across my forehead—from what, I don't know. A chunk was missing from the tip of my nose from all of my weight bearing down on an incorrectly-placed breathing mask during my many days lying facedown. My right ear was red and looked like it had been chewed on by a dog. My left cheek had a large gouge in it, just below my jawline, and under that was another scar. As I stood up, I saw my body. My

270-pound body, forged from years of lifting huge amounts of weight, was gone, replaced by skin and bones. All I could see were bones. My chest was gone, and all I could see was my sternum poking through the skin on my torso. I had a bandage on my throat where the trach had been. I also had three large indentations that looked like gunshot wounds over my ribs. I had a huge surgery scar under my right pectoral muscle, where they had opened me up and cleaned me out multiple times when my chest cavity had started to fill with blood,. I gave myself a minute to take it all in and then took my shower. I would use this image of myself as motivation.

The first time I brushed my teeth in rehab I only had the coordination to hold onto the brush and move my head back and forth to clean my teeth. I almost accepted that I would have to use this method from now on. Things were different, and I guess I just had to accept them. Now, though, my mindset had changed. I would no longer accept these new ways of doing things. I would force my body to respond and act "normal" again. I had to do every action with purpose now. No more letting my body do what it wanted to do because it was weak. I started to force myself to do the "proper" movements. I got dressed that day without the use of those assistance devices. It took a while and I was late for my next session, but they would never come out of that closet again. No matter what I had to do or how long it took me to get dressed, I would never use those assistance devices again.

[9]
MENTALLY BROKE

I was only in rehab for just under three weeks, but a lot happened during that time that made a big impact on my life. For one, I asked Melinda to marry me. She had called me and told me she was going by our house to grab a few things. She only went back to the house a few times while I was in the hospital because she said it upset her too much. This time, I wanted her to have a good experience at the house. I told her there was something else I needed her to grab while she was there but didn't tell her what it was, just where to look. When I got a phone call a few minutes later, I could hardly understand her. She had found her ring. I had gotten it before I got sick, but at that time, I didn't have a plan yet on when I would give it to her. I just knew I wanted to marry her. It may not have been the best timing or the most romantic way to propose, but after everything we had been through, I wanted her to know how much I loved and cared about her. I wanted her to have something positive in her life after all the suffering. Although I couldn't get down on one knee or really even stand, I asked her to marry me when she got back to the rehab center. And she said yes.

I was making a lot of progress. I had been given specific tasks that had to be completed if I wanted to be officially released from the rehab program. I was starting to work on skills I would need to get through everyday life. I had gotten to the point where I could get up from my wheelchair without assistance, move to the back of the chair (small shuffle steps), remove the portable oxygen tank, replace it with a new one, and then get back into the chair. I thought this was the biggest accomplishment! The oxygen tank had to be lifted straight up to get it out of the holder it was in, and it felt like it weighed a thousand pounds. Watching the physical therapist walk through the exercise, I was in awe of her strength. She lifted the tank like it was nothing! This was one of the times when I watched "normal" people completing "normal" tasks and envied them. I almost couldn't remember a time when I was able-bodied. Nonetheless, I was excited with my progress, but I was worried. I was still on oxygen twenty-four hours a day. I still required assistance with many basic tasks. Hell, I was still on blood-thinners and was worried that if I fell I would bleed to death. I had already fallen twice in the bathroom (Not that anyone knew, though) and had some bad welts on my arms that I kept hidden. I did a few things in rehab that worried and pissed off the staff and my family; things I wasn't supposed to do because they felt it was too dangerous. I wouldn't stop pushing myself, so I kept my mouth shut and the sleeves on my shirt pulled down.

One day, I asked if I could "free walk," a term I had made up myself. My physical therapist for the day said she'd never heard it referred to as "free walking" but guessed it was an accurate way to describe it. I had been walking since day one in rehab but not without the assistance of staff and a mobility device. I wanted to walk like everyone else. I was scared to death but so excited at the same time. Part of it was the fear of falling, but mostly I was scared that I wouldn't be able to walk again like I had before.

Even though it had only been months since I had walked without any aid, it felt like I had waited years for this. I remember the moment like it just happened, and I get choked up thinking about it. I was seated in my wheelchair in front of the walking bars: two metal pipes about four feet high that allow a person to walk between, holding on to the bars for balance. I decided to use them differently. I stood up and began to walk along the outside of the bars. I thought if I really needed them, I could grab onto at least one bar for balance. They also served as a measure of how far I had gone and gave me a distance goal so I could say I "finished" after I got all the way around them. As I was walking, I felt so unbalanced and awkward, but I didn't care. I knew people were watching me, but I didn't care. I was walking again and with no walker! Melinda was there watching me. I made the corner along one side of the walking bars, made the straightaway, and then rounded the last corner. As I pushed toward the finish (making it back to my wheelchair), I began to get short of breath, but I pushed on. Compelled by a combination of fear that I would fall and hurt myself and joy from how far I had come in such a short period of time, I made it back to my chair. I made sure I sat down with some control and didn't just plop back into place. I was so happy and proud of myself. I couldn't believe what I had just done! It was everything I had been thinking about and hoping for since waking up!

I once watched a documentary in which a young man who had been paralyzed in a car accident and had also lost function in his hands had a recurring dream of breaking free from his wheelchair and recovering the use of his legs. In his dreams, he would wake up and float up out of bed into the sky. His legs and hands would then change back to normal again and work like everyone else's. He said it made him feel free. He would fly around doing anything he wanted, but in the end each time, he would wake up to his broken body, not able to walk and not able to use his hands properly. I had a similar dream once in rehab. I dreamed I woke up in my hospital bed, yawned and stretched like I used to, threw my feet over the side of the bed, then sat up and waited until I woke up enough to stand. I then stood and walked to the bathroom to begin my usual morning ritual to begin the day. Everything was open to me. There were no limitations. I was strong again. I looked normal again and had no scars. My hair wasn't thin and falling out. I could speak with a strong voice like I used to. I no longer was in pain, and I didn't need to use an oxygen machine. I could protect and take care of Melinda again. It seemed so real, but I woke up like I had been waking up since coming out of my coma. I woke up to a dark, cold hospital room, banging on the side rail for Melinda to wake up, disturbing her sleep just so she could help me stand to piss into a bed pan under a makeshift toilet, which she then had to dump in the toilet in the bathroom! For the first time, I began to feel deeply depressed. This is what my life had become. I was slowly starting to feel trapped in my body with no hope of being what I was before. This was my new normal.

Up to this point, I had never really felt depressed or felt sorry for myself for long. I was glad to be alive, and everyone around me was so positive and happy that it was hard to get down. Things were different now. I wasn't healing like I wanted to. Every day, people told me that I was a miracle and that my recovery was coming along so fast, but for me, it wasn't fast enough. When I showed my physical therapists a video online of me powerlifting, they couldn't believe it was me. I no longer looked like the strong man in the video. Sometimes the mental image we hold of ourselves isn't the person other people see. I had thought of myself as a big, strong guy. But the man I thought I was—he was no longer the man people saw. I looked at myself in the mirror and tried to take an unbiased assessment of myself. What did I really look like when people saw me? I didn't like what I saw. Not only did I look weak, but I looked like someone a bully would be ashamed to mess with. Seeing yourself so differently from almost one day to the next can mess with your mind. One moment, I was functioning perfectly, and then the next instant, my total outlook on life, and how I had to handle and approach it, completely changed.

I knew I was very lucky to be in the condition I was in at the time. There was a man in rehab who had lost his left leg from the knee down. He was wheeled into rehab every day and would just stare at the floor. The most I saw him do was play a board game to show hand dexterity. His injury was permanent, and he was truly depressed. I could have lost my right arm and left leg to blood clots, but I didn't. In the past I would have viewed him as someone who had given up and needed to get his head on straight. Where I was mentally now, though, I could easily understand where he was and why.

I was also having issues dealing with things that had happened to me while on the job as a patrol officer. Experiences I had stuffed in the back of my mind so I could sleep at night and function properly started to surface. Anyone who has worked in law enforcement for any length of time has undoubtedly seen some horrible stuff and has probably been in some God-awful situations. Many have probably also buried those experiences in the back of their minds to allow themselves to keep on going. If faced with a small percentage of what police officers see every day, most people would walk away from the job and seek professional counseling for the rest of their lives. We don't do that, though. Even when faced with complete tragedy, we push on with no help. Even in this day and age, if you seek counseling you are seen as weak and possibly unfit for the job. This is sad and a crime to our profession and the mental health of our officers, but it's the reality of it. When an officer I had worked with for years shot and killed himself due to depression, for the first and only time I can remember, a counselor was made available to anyone who needed to talk. One of the supervisors actually laughed and made the statement that if you were one of the weak people that needed to go cry to a quack then you could go after your shift was over. This is the police culture.

I had pushed down all the things I had seen, but it was all coming to the surface now. I asked for someone to speak with, and they brought in a lady who said she was a trained counselor and would help me if I wanted to talk. I started to tell her of a few things that had happened to me at work that I had never dealt with, hoping she would give me a coping technique, advice, or some way to deal with what was going on in my head. All she did was stare at me with a look of disbelief on her face. I could see that what I was telling her was so foreign and almost unbelievable that she was no longer listening in a professional capacity but more out of morbid curiosity. The reality of a veteran police officer is not the same as that of an average citizen. Even for a person like this counselor who was supposedly trained to help people with mental issues, the horrific memories can be hard to hear. It did help to verbalize some of the things that gave me issues and nightmares, but the counselor was of no help. A few days later, I asked for someone else, but the outcome was the same: wide eyes and silence. I decided to bottle everything back up and continue on, which wasn't a solution at all.

I felt myself getting physically ill. I thought I had the flu again or something similar. Looking back, I think I was making myself ill from stress. My eating slowed down, and I started to lose weight again. I had only gained around ten pounds since waking up, but I was getting thinner again. I started to show up to my PT sessions late and without the drive I had before. The wound on my backside got worse and smelled horrible. I feared it would soon turn septic. It didn't help that no one really seemed to know how to change the bandages properly. Staff had to change the bandages three times a week, and many times, they seemed to be guessing as to how to properly dress the wound. It seems crazy that a rehab center staffed with doctors and nurses wouldn't know how to treat a patient's wounds, but this is the sad, scary reality in some facilities. Naturally, this added to my stress levels as well. How could I get better if the freaking staff didn't even know how to dress my wounds?!? I would have tried to do it myself if I could have reached back there—that's how bad it was.

I couldn't take it all anymore, so I spoke to my doctor and told him that I wanted to go home. I said that I felt I was becoming depressed and my progress was going backwards because of it. I said I needed to finish my rehab at home. He actually agreed but advised me to stay in rehab a while longer until I could become a bit more independent.

Even though I wanted to leave rehab, I was scared at the thought of it. I couldn't imagine being alone at home. What if I had an issue with my oxygen? What if I had problems with my wound? Would it get infected, turn septic, and kill me? Who would help me if I needed it? Melinda would be at home only half the day. There would be no way an ambulance could get to me in time, if I were even able to call 911. I would probably be dead by the time they got to me. There were so many variables, but I knew I had to leave.

The doctor finally gave me a release date. It was written on the whiteboard in my room, along with all of my medical information. I announced it to everyone that came to visit. I was so happy, and they were all proud of me. I couldn't wait to sleep in my own bed, use my own shower, and eat food from my own kitchen.

I wheeled myself into the room for my last scheduled PT session. I was the only one there that day; it was strangely quiet. As my trainer started to gather the equipment for my last workout, I sat in my wheelchair and looked around the room and started to cry. I'm not sure exactly what triggered my reaction, but these certainly weren't tears of joy. It was complete exhaustion. Everything had caught up to me and was now coming out. All the years of seeing horrible things while working patrol, all the stress from my sickness, all of the emotion of the good and the bad things from being in the hospital and now recovery—it all came out. I was so embarrassed. Here I was again, not who I thought I was. I was a sick, weak person in a wheelchair, crying like a baby right in front of people. I was handed a box of tissues and told my PT for the day would be to wheel myself around the facility and try to compose myself. I was grateful for the reprieve. I wheeled myself down the hall to the large double glass doors that opened to the field at the back of the facility. I sat, looking out over the field, and cried.

The field was beautiful to me. I had gone out there one time to visit with some supervisors from work. Also, a week or so before, one of the patient's daughters had held her wedding out there. On this particular day, it was warm, and the sun was shining through the glass doors onto the floor. I wheeled myself into the warm sunlight and just sat there crying. It felt good to get it out. It felt good to cry. I'm not sure how long I sat there—twenty minutes, maybe thirty. Eventually, my physical therapist walked up and asked if I was okay. I told her I was and just needed a few more minutes alone. She said my training was over and when I was ready, I should wheel myself back to my room. I stayed a few more minutes, composed myself, and then wheeled myself back to my room to wash my face.

This mental breakdown would be the first of many, if I'm going to be completely honest. We try to be tough. We try to be superhuman. We pretend that once we've cried we have gotten everything out of our system and are good to move on—it's done and over. But this is a lie. Until we deal with our issues properly, they continue to haunt us. Even then, there's no guarantee that they may not return, because these feelings, these issues, are recurring. They keep coming back. I know this has been my experience. I'm okay at putting on a good face for people, but it is only that: a face. It's not the real person or how I truly feel.

I would get out of rehab later in the same week as my breakdown. And I walked out of that facility. I had practiced getting into my truck a few times. Melinda drove my pickup every once in a while to make sure it didn't sit too long without running. It was actually easier to boost myself up into the passenger seat of the pickup than to drop down into a low car. On the day I was released, I was wheeled to the front doors of the facility, with the pickup waiting just outside. Melinda was there, of course, as was her sister. I stood up and walked out the door to the pickup. With a little help, I boosted myself into the passenger seat and strapped myself in for the ride. After speaking briefly to Melinda's sister, we were off.

There were many things to take care of on this day that worried me, such as meeting the home healthcare company at my house to set up the home oxygen condenser and get extra portable tanks. (I only had about an hour's worth of oxygen in the tank I was on.) The police association was hosting fundraisers for me at multiple restaurants, and a lot of people were going to be there. I also had family coming to the house to welcome me home, but once I got in the pickup and we started off down the road, all of these thoughts went out of my head. A trip home in your own truck may seem like such a small thing, but to me, it was huge. I was seeing the outside world for the first time in months. I looked with child-like wonder at everything around me. I don't remember if Melinda and I even talked. I just remember looking at the trees and the sunshine; the people in the passing cars; everyone going about their everyday lives, not knowing how close the person next to them had come to no longer being on this earth. Not that I was anyone special for them to marvel at, but it's funny how you never really know the stories of the people next to you in traffic, what they have been through and why they might be staring off into space or staring at you. It's difficult for me to describe what captured my attention so much. Being told your life is over, that you will soon die...suddenly the small things seem to mean so much more. If you were told today that tomorrow you would lose your freedom forever, I'm sure small things like sitting on the porch and watching it rain or driving in a car with the window rolled down, enjoying feeling the sun on your skin, would hold more value. Things you had previously taken for granted would suddenly become more important, and I bet you wouldn't be able to get enough of them. That's what it felt like to me, but I was coming out the other side. I hadn't known I would be kept from these simple things for so long, but now that I was released to spend my days as I wished, these simple things became everything to me. The sun and the trees—to this day, these are two things that I still stop and watch and am amazed by.

Before I knew it, we were home. The oxygen arrived, and so did my family and friends. I sat on the couch for a brief period of time but quickly made my way to my bed to rest, which felt like heaven to me. I was so happy to be home. For now, everything was perfect, but it wouldn't last. Soon, the depression and negative thoughts would return and the struggles would begin again, even worse than before. For right now, though, I was happy, and I would enjoy it.

THE WEDDING

MELINDA and I had thought about what kind of wedding we wanted. We were offered large venues to have the wedding at by churches that wanted to help and donate their time and services. At first, we thought this would be a great idea. Everyone who had supported me could attend, and we would make it a huge celebration! One church even wanted to create a live satellite feed so members who had heard about my story every Sunday could watch from home. Even though I was a very private person, this did not bother me. I wanted everyone to share in the day when Melinda and I got married and to finally see me healthier and able to walk. The reality of things, though, set in, and even with a donated venue, the cost on our end was going to be more than we could afford. Also, we didn't want to wait that long to get married. We were living (as we saw it) outside of what God wanted for us. After everything that God had done for us, all of the prayers answered and blessings given to us, we felt like hypocrites by waiting another six or so months to get married while already living together. One of the churches that helped a lot during my illness and where I had also worked as part-time security for years offered the use of one of their private rooms to have a very small and short ceremony. We quickly agreed and set the date for only a week later.

April 13, 2014, was the date we would be married. I can't remember what I wore or what Melinda wore, and for some reason, no pictures were taken. I guess we were too caught up to remind someone to bring a camera. I remember, though, that it was a cold, windy, and rainy day. Melinda and I drove to the church that morning and parked as close as we could to the main entrance. It was probably only about fifty yards to the front door, but to me, it looked like a mile. I was determined, though, to make it without having to stop. I refused to use my walker and just had my portable oxygen tank on wheels to push. As I got out of the car, I was almost knocked over by the wind, which was something I had yet to prepare for in therapy. My balance was still off, so the wind added another challenge. As I stood next to the car, I looked up, saw the distance I had to go, then put my head down and started walking. It seemed to take forever, but I finally made it to the main entrance and inside the church. Quickly, I found a chair just inside the doors and crashed down. I was so tired but happy I had made it. I had yet to have walked that distance without a break. I sat and waited briefly for our friends who would serve as witnesses to arrive. The pastor facilitating the ceremony walked over to us a short time later to go over anything we would need. I told him I wanted a chair to sit on while he was talking but that I wanted to stand when I put the ring on Melinda's finger. Melinda was kind enough to request a chair for both of us so that I wouldn't feel embarrassed being the only one sitting. After making the arrangements, we were shown to the nearby room where our wedding would take place. The room was small but set up very nicely.

———

As the ceremony started, I began to get more nervous. I was only halfway listening to what the pastor was saying because I was concentrating on what I was about to have to do. I started to sweat profusely. I was getting hot, and my breathing was becoming shallower. This wasn't good. I would soon have to stand, and I needed to be relaxed and in control of my breathing. I tried desperately to calm myself, but it was no use. The sweating becoming more pronounced, and I was turning bright red. The time finally came for us to exchange our rings. I struggled a bit but was able to stand without rocking to gain momentum or without any assistance. I also decided to take my oxygen off. I didn't want my wife or anyone else to see me getting married looking like that. I wanted my wife to see me as a whole man who didn't need a medical device to stand before her. I would either get through it or pass out trying, but I wasn't going to have a tube sticking out of my nose when I looked at Melinda and she looked back at me during this special moment. As the pastor spoke, Melinda and I held hands and looked at each other. I couldn't believe this was finally happening. This wasn't at all as I had imagined it, but I was still thankful. When Melinda slipped the ring on my finger and the pastor began to speak again, I felt exhaustion start to kick in. My breathing became more labored. I was almost done and could sit down soon. I tried to focus on one single point and concentrate like they had taught me in the hospital, something to help me calm down and control my breathing. To keep everyone from seeing my face, I looked down at Melinda's hand. I must have been six shades of purple and dripping with sweat. I breathed deliberately: in through my nose, pause, then out through my mouth. I was waiting for the pastor to finish so I could put the ring on Melinda's finger. I was hoping he would see me struggling and realize he needed to hurry up, but he didn't. It seemed like he went on forever! I started to get dizzy. I was actually starting to get a bit angry at the situation. How could he not know there was no way I could stand this long? My legs started to give out, so I locked them and hoped I didn't pass out and take a header straight to the floor or into my new bride, knocking her over in the process. Finally, he finished and I could place the ring on Melinda's finger! My hand shook as I held her hand and tried to place the ring on her finger. I got it about halfway on when my legs gave out. I fell toward the chair and, luckily, landed butt-first into it. I had accomplished my goal! I had stood during the ring portion of my wedding ceremony and placed the ring on my bride's finger, albeit only halfway.

Sadly enough, I don't recall what happened afterwards, whether we went back home or to a restaurant or what we did, but at least I do remember the important part: Melinda and I were finally married, and now we would be living correctly in front of God. And that made me happy.

[11]
THE START OF NORMAL

I DON'T REMEMBER a honeymoon period after the wedding. There certainly wasn't an actual honeymoon. We had too many expenses from medical bills and treatments for us to afford one. I also had too many doctor appointments and checkups to be able to leave for a week. But I don't remember a figurative honeymoon period either, a time when we were both simply happy and care-free. Maybe it was my mental state or how I felt at the time, but I only remember dark times. I doubt that most people have truly faced who they are. They may have an idea of who they would like to be and who other people think they are, but truly facing yourself can destroy a person. During this time, this is what I was going through, and it almost broke me. It almost broke up my new marriage, as well.

A few times a week, nurses came to the house to care for my wounds. (I still had a wound vac hooked up to my back and two giant wounds on my heels that had to be looked after.) When Melinda got up around 5:00 a.m. to leave for work, she made sure I got from the bedroom to the living room. The oxygen condenser had a tube long enough to reach into the living room and allowed me to be a bit more mobile around the first floor of the house. I would normally just stick to sitting or lying on the couch. Melinda would set out my pills for the morning and make me breakfast. Because the supplemental oxygen in close proximity to the microwave or oven could set off an explosion, I wasn't allowed to go into the kitchen. I wasn't that worried, but it scared Melinda, so I stayed away from the kitchen. After getting me set for the day, Melinda would kiss me goodbye, and I would fall asleep on the couch. Normally, I didn't have an appetite and would fall asleep without eating. Usually, though, Melinda would call about an hour later to check on me, and I would try to force some food down then after assuring her that I had already eaten and taken all my pills. I was on so many pain-killers it was a wonder I was able to eat anything.

Melinda would give me small tasks to accomplish while she was gone, but I couldn't seem to get them done by the time she got home. They would be something small like going through the large stack of mail which had accumulated over the months I was hospitalized and sorting the junk mail from the mail that needed to be handled, like bills or medical paperwork. I couldn't get it done, though. I thought, initially, that maybe I was just tired and needed to rest. Maybe I just wasn't used to waking up in the morning and working on a project. It's not like I had ever really been great at paperwork to begin with. After time went on, though, I realized that no matter what task Melinda gave me, I couldn't stay awake to complete it. It felt strange. I had always been a motivated person, but I just couldn't get that spark to move. I just wanted to sleep. At first, Melinda was fine with me sleeping while she was gone, but slowly, she started to question what I had been doing all day. I felt like such a loser. I didn't know why I couldn't stay awake, nor did I know why I just didn't seem to care.

I also noticed I was becoming more dependent on the pain

medication I had been prescribed. In the hospital, I had been adamant about not getting too dependent on the pain meds. Once, I had even asked to discontinue some of the meds because I didn't want to get hooked on them. Because of the severity of the pain, this didn't last very long, but at least I was able to lower the dosages. Now, though, I was becoming totally dependent on all of the pain meds. I would take pills in the morning, in the afternoon, and in the evening before bed. Every morning when I woke up, I felt like I had been hit by a truck. I would take my pills, start to feel better, and drift off to sleep. Around three in the afternoon, I would start feeling the pain resurface. When I would tell Melinda that I wasn't feeling well, she would remind me when my next dosage was due. I went from waiting until the proper time to coming up with reasons why I needed my meds early. I started to become angry and verbally abusive toward Melinda. I would yell and slam things; to get my meds, I would act out to show how much pain I was in. Melinda tried to be calm with me. She tried to understand, but after a while, even she became short with me. How could she not? She never yelled at me, nor was she ever mean, but I could tell my attitude was starting to wear on her.

One day, while sitting on the couch going through papers I had been left to sort, I found a bag from the pharmacy with a breakdown of all the medication I was taking, along with a description of what they did and their side effects. I was taking Valium, oxycodone, Xanax, and wearing a fentanyl patch, along with taking a blood thinner, a pill for my heart, and a pill for acid reflux. Almost every one of them had a side effect of appetite suppression. They could also make people drowsy and kill their libido. I'm not sure why it didn't occur to me sooner to think maybe the medication had something to do with why I was acting differently; probably because nothing felt normal to me at this time. I didn't even remember what it felt like to be normal. I forgot what normal day-to-day discomforts felt like. I was either doped up, feeling nothing, or in horrible pain. Those were my two extremes.

Aside from the very end of rehab, my attitude was fine while I was hospitalized. I thought I had done a great job of staying motivated and pushing hard to get better. A lot had changed from that time to what was going on now that I was home. It was becoming quite clear that things were not good, possibly because of the pills I was taking or how I was taking them. The pills were affecting me in a negative way and causing issues with my marriage, but I didn't stop taking them right away.

One afternoon, Melinda and I were in an all-you-can-eat sushi restaurant where we used to go at least twice a week before I got sick. Prior to getting sick, I would eat around eight or nine rolls; now I could barely finish one. Melinda was trying so hard to be supportive, but she was getting worn down by this time. We had ventured out to the restaurant during the afternoon to avoid the crowds and make me feel more comfortable. I was still using my oxygen tank and still had a wound vac attached to my back and didn't always deal well with the stares I got out in public. At first, it really didn't bother me, but as time went on, it started to wear on me.

I had, once again, ordered a single roll and barely finished it. Melinda was trying to tell me how concerned she was about me and my attitude. As she was talking, a group of people passed by our table. They glanced at me briefly and continued on. Then they started laughing. This pissed me off. I felt like I was being viewed as some oddity, like I was being disrespected. I told her I was tired of being looked at like a freak, and I wished I had the strength to get up and confront the people. She looked as if she were going to cry. She told me that I had a crazy look on my face and that was why I was being stared at, not because of my oxygen tank or wound vac—not even because of my sickly, skinny appearance. It was how I was carrying myself and the expressions on my face. It was probably all she could do to keep from yelling at me. I just laughed, though, and looked down at my plate. What she was saying didn't sink in then, but the comment sure hit home. "You look crazy"...that stuck with me.

I was convinced that people around me were just being mean, staring at me and laughing to themselves about how pathetic I looked. Sure, I bet it caught people's eyes to see a stick-skinny, six foot three guy with a portable oxygen tank and a device that looked like a purse with a tube extending from it, connecting to something in the back of his pants; but what they ended up looking at was the way I was carrying myself. I just didn't realize it at the time. Even if I had been back to normal physically, I'm sure people would have stared at me, simply because of how I was presenting myself. I had given in to what I had become in my mind. I was broken; I was angry. I was not myself. I no longer cared to try and make myself presentable in public. I had fallen into the role of a person with a great illness. It oozed from every pore in me. I talked with a slow, slurred speech. I sat with my shoulders hunched forward and my head and neck jutting out. I wouldn't even cover my mouth when I coughed or wipe food from my mouth or chin when I ate. I was a sick person, and sick people didn't do these things. I was to be pitied and felt sorry for—to some extent, the way I had been treated in the hospital. I failed to realize that, even though I was sick, I was in no way as helpless as the person I had been only a month or so earlier. Couple the physical attributes of a severely sick person with the mentality of a disturbed and angry person, and the combination can be startling. I didn't allow everyone to see me like this, but I made sure Melinda got the full effect of the "new me," and it was troubling to her. Show that same character to a stranger walking past and they will stare for sure.

I had never been especially social or one who enjoyed going

out much, but before I got sick, I would at least try things with Melinda before totally ruling them out. Now, I stubbornly said no in favor of either lying in bed or on the couch. One particular argument (most likely over leaving the house) ended with her walking out of the room, asking, "Where did the man go that I fell in love with?" This crushed me. People can fool themselves into thinking everything is okay or that their actions are justified. They think everyone else around them is the problem, or possibly that the people around them don't care enough to show compassion and be more supportive. Many times, though, that kind of thought process is not based in reality. These are excuses justified in their minds to give validation to how they are acting. This is what I was doing. I was blaming the one person who had stuck by my side through the worst of times. When anyone else would have left and continued on with her life—gone and found another boyfriend to enjoy things with, to love and have fun and be active with—Melinda chose to stay with her sick boyfriend. And now I was pushing her away and treating her so wrongly after everything she had done. This would prove to be another turning point for me. I decided to no longer take pain pills like I had been. No longer would I use my illness as an excuse for my bad attitude. For everything she had done for me, I would try to make her life as good as she deserved it to be.

It took approximately two days to get past the worst of the withdrawal symptoms. Directly after our argument resulting in my decision, I told Melinda that I was coming off all of my pain medicine and that I just wanted to be left alone in the bedroom. Maybe it would have been wiser to have finished out that day and to have started fresh in the morning, but I felt like there was no time like the present, and if I waited another day my will might not be as strong. I might as well get the pain over with as soon as possible. It was approaching mid-afternoon, and I could tell things were about to get bad. As usual, when I was due for a dose of my pills, the flu symptoms started. To take my mind off the ever-increasing pain, I tried to watch television. Thinking over what Melinda had said to me, my emotions were certainly amplified, and I started thinking about all of the issues we had been having since I got out of the hospital. I thought of everything that Melinda had sacrificed for me and how poorly I had treated her in return. I began to cry, out of sadness as well as rage at myself for the situation I had created. Then the pain became worse. Without thinking, I started to kick my legs to the side like a newborn child does. Somehow, this served as a comforting mechanism. I began to gnash my teeth and breathe heavily. The pain was increasing still. I had a box of tissues next to me in the bed, and I grabbed them with my right hand. I began to squeeze the box as hard as I could—anything to take my mind off the pain. This was a different kind of pain from that of a twisted ankle or broken leg, where the pain is localized in a specific area. This was a full-body sensation. This was a combination of feeling emotionally confused, head-to-toe pain, and a claustrophobic, suffocating feeling. Next, I felt a compression on my chest, and I kicked my legs more. I thought maybe I was having a heart attack! My heartbeats seemed so loud I almost couldn't hear anything else. I writhed in pain, gripping the tissue box and kicking my legs, gnashing my teeth together still. This continued in cycles, with my body going into spasms for a while, then relaxing. I'm not sure if the spasms would end or my body would just give out. When I felt on the verge of giving in to the intense desire to end my suffering by swallowing the pain pills, I would think about the way I had acted toward Melinda, and this gave me the strength to continue on for a few more minutes. The pain began to come in more frequent waves, and I knew things were about to get even worse. Again, I felt like I couldn't breathe, but this time, the sensation was worse. Somehow, I sensed that there was no point in reaching for my oxygen. This was something coming from inside that the oxygen machine couldn't help alleviate, something that my body was causing and an oxygen condenser couldn't fix. Melinda came in at some point and saw me kicking and holding the now completely crushed tissue box with my right hand. She tried to comfort me and take the box away. Through clinched teeth, gritting through the pain and discomfort, I asked her to go away. She looked concerned but seemed to have an understanding of what was happening. Although she left the room and continued to look in on me, she never interrupted the process. She knew it was something I needed to endure to come out on the other end as "me" again.

I didn't sleep that night, not much at least, but at some point, I passed out. I was covered in sweat with all of the covers kicked off of me. The pillows were strewn about the room. Sometime during the night, Melinda covered me up and climbed into bed and fell asleep next to me. When I woke up, the pain was still there but was somewhat different because now I felt nauseated. I began to cough, and my throat began to spasm. I started to feel like I was hyperventilating. I couldn't get control of my breathing. Out of instinct, I sat up quickly, gasping for breath. I desperately tried to grab a deep breath, but it was no use, and I began to get scared. I couldn't breathe! I made horrible, loud, gasping sounds as I tried to inhale. I stood up and leaned on the side of the bed, shaking my head from side to side, saying "no" in between gasps. The word was barely intelligible because I didn't have the air. I was saying no to passing out like this, to dying like this. This lasted for far too long. I dropped to my knees, no longer able to speak. My chest was on fire from the convulsions. I pulled in my breath hard, one last time, and tried to hold it, tried to control the contractions. Air! I was finally able to exhale and let the pressure off. Air! I was finally able to take in a shallow, life-saving breath. Air! I was finally able to form the word "slow" in an attempt to trick myself into slowing down my breathing to gain back some control. "Slow." I repeated it again. "Slow." Over and over again. Every time I was able to get the word out, I gained a little more control of my breathing. When I looked up from my position on the floor, Melinda was by my side. She had the phone in her hand and was calling 911. Tears rolled down my face, and my throat and chest burned. I suddenly felt as if I was going to vomit. I quickly jumped up and made my way to the bathroom sink. Just in time, I vomited into the sink, creating another great release of pressure. I was so embarrassed and scared by what had just happened. Typical of Melinda, she put aside her own feelings and, without hesitation, took care of me, cleaning up after me and helping me back to bed. She comforted me afterwards and later said she had been awakened by me gasping for air, which lasted approximately five minutes. She was calling 911 when I finally fell to the ground and started to pass out. She said I was turning purple and my eyes were bugging out. She cried afterwards from the fear of losing me but had remained strong and composed when I had needed her to be.

By the next day the pain was back down to a manageable, dull flu feeling. I knew I needed to get some sleep once night came. I'm not going to lie and say that I kicked all of my pain meds cold turkey like I had intended—I wasn't that tough. That second day, I made it all the way to about 9:00 p.m. before Melinda was kind enough to suggest I take a pill to take the edge off in hope of getting a good night's rest. I was still experiencing flashbacks and waking up in our bed thinking I was back in the hospital. I would jump up in the middle of the night in the midst of a panic attack and would go into the bathroom or a corner and cower, sobbing until I was able to compose myself. Instead of going back to bed, I would usually stay up all night, mindlessly watching TV to try and settle my mind. To help avoid these occurrences, I started to take my Xanax at night before bed, although they still happened on occasion.

By the third day, I started to feel as though I was coming out the other side of the withdrawal. There were no birds chirping, and I didn't feel like dancing or going out on the town, but I also didn't feel numb to the world, nor did I feel like sleeping all day. This would be the start of getting "me" back...the start of getting back to normal.

[12]
VIOLENCE OF ACTION

Anger is a big motivator for me; it always has been. Years ago, I started writing down sayings that inspired me in a small spiral notebook that I kept close by and would use to get myself in the right mindset for whatever I was doing at the time. Over the years, my motivation technique evolved into using music or a saved speech on an MP3 device that I could quickly pull up and listen to. As a police officer, I carried an MP3 player with me every day to work. I made a clip that I mounted in my patrol car just below the A/C vents that allowed me to easily manipulate the player while I was driving. Normally, I would just have music playing in the background, but if a hot call came over the radio I would quickly flip to something that woke me up and got me focused. You would think the call alone would do that, but when working over twelve-hour shifts, you have a tendency to get tired and need a boost at times. Sometimes, if I felt something was really speaking to me, I would tape a quote to the dashboard. One particular quote I liked to have around was, "What would you attempt to do if you knew you could not fail?" When I trained recruits to be police officers and they were having a particularly difficult time getting their confidence up to handle a call on the street I would share this quote with them, hoping it would give them the freedom to forget about failure or looking stupid and concentrate instead on performing to the best of their abilities. There is a great freedom in not worrying about what anyone else thinks of you and just doing what you know you can do. Another saying that I kept nearby was, "violence of action." In police work, you may sit for hours on end in your patrol car, not doing much of anything, then when you least expect it, you get dispatched to a dangerous call that requires you to be immediately switched on. Situations arise where you know you are going to be fighting with someone who is drunk, high on drugs, or just plain pissed off, and you have to match their aggressiveness. Sometimes, even the best of us have trouble getting our mind right, knowing that in seconds, we'll be in the fight of our lives; and having something like this to rev me up has always helped me. To get me back on track with my training, I needed to return to this process once again.

Even though I was off my pain meds now, my motivation for doing my physical therapy was still lagging. At first, the same regimen I had followed in the hospital was something I could really sink my teeth into, but now things had grown stale. I needed something to get me going. I realized that if I wanted to perform the way I used to, I would have to employ the tactics that had worked for me in the past. I got my MP3 player out and started listening to the songs that motivated me. I started listening, on a consistent basis, to the speeches that really hit home for me. I started arranging workout sessions with my buddies so that I had to put the work in and couldn't quit. They wouldn't let me quit, even if I wanted to.

I remember the first sleepless night when, instead of sitting up all night watching TV, I decided to take a step down the road that would put my body back in working order. It was probably around 11:00 at night. Melinda was long since asleep in the bed next to me. I quietly rolled out of bed, disconnected from the home oxygen unit by the bed, grabbed my portable oxygen tank, and rolled it out of the room and down the hall toward the garage. I plugged my MP3 player into the stereo and sat in front of the dumbbell rack. My shoulders were so weak. I had never had very broad shoulders, but I had built them up over time. Now, my shoulders were narrow and sloped. This is where I would start. With my oxygen tank a safe distance away, I could sit down and do shoulder raises. To start with, I used nothing more than my own body weight, lifting my arms in front of me and then to the side. Next, I grabbed the 2.5-lb. plates. I set a rep range and started to lift the weights. I had the radio turned up and was sure Melinda would hear the racket and come to investigate fairly quickly, but she was sleeping soundly. I made it up to 5-lb. dumbbells that first night—a sad amount of weight. But from where I was coming from, I had to be satisfied, at least for this session. With the same weights, I worked my way into dumbbell curls and shrugs—all exercises I could do from the same seated position. As I went from one exercise to the next, I noticed something was not right. I used to feel a rush from training. I used to feel the endorphins surging through my body, and it was a great high. I could feel my muscles contracting and growing as I went. The music motivated me, and I could go for hours. Now, though, it was like I was just going through the motions. I used to be puzzled by those kinds of guys at the gym—why were they wasting their time going through the same routine with no motivation and no feeling? No wonder they got little to no results. They weren't even trying. Now I was experiencing this in my own workout. I was just going through the motions. Pick the weight up. Put it down. Pick the weight up. Put it down. Count from one to ten, then rest. It was a letdown. I couldn't stop, though. I had to get my strength back. I had to get my body back. I had to get back to who I was before all of this happened—or at least as close as possible.

I picked the weights up and started in on another set of front raises. This time, I would push harder. This time, I wouldn't quit when I started to feel short of breath. This time, I would fight through the pain like I used to. I wouldn't get scared when my breathing became labored. I would control my breathing like I had been trained to do. As I watched my form in the mirror, hoping I would see some hint of a muscle flexing in my shoulders, the garage door to the house opened. Melinda was angry. She came into the garage, yelling at me, "Do you know how scared you made me? Do you know the thoughts going through my head when I woke up and you were gone?" She had every right to be upset, but this time, she would have to accept what I was doing. I told her that I wasn't going to sit inside anymore, wasting away. I was going to get back to where I was before, and that meant training and working on me. She questioned the safety of what I was doing alone in the garage. What if one of the weights fell on me? What if the oxygen tank hit the floor and exploded? She went through every possible scenario, but I wasn't going to let it stop me. I told her I was almost done and would be back in bed soon enough. I finished my sad little workout that night and went back to bed.

From that day on, I pushed myself harder with every work-out. A good friend, whom I had wrestled and boxed with before becoming ill, started coming over once a week to help me with my conditioning by putting me through a boxing workout. I would hit mitts for twenty-second rounds for as many rounds as I could. I increased the round lengths every session. I also got more involved in weight training again by having a few guys from work come by and lift weights in my garage. These sessions really helped get my mind right and helped to push me into that next gear. I began to dead lift and squat again as well. I was still going to wound therapy twice a week and still had my wound vac on, too. Every weightlifting session, I tore open my wounds and had to face the doctors when I got to wound therapy. They were trying to get the wounds on my heels and back to close, but every week, I was tearing them back open by training. The staff weren't the least bit happy with me, but I didn't care. I told them I *had* to *move*. I had to work out. I had to lift weights. I was even beginning to put body weight back on, and I wasn't about to lose the gains that I had made by lying around the house again, waiting months, possibly, for my wounds to heal.

Lugging around the wound vac still bothered me mentally. Wearing it made me feel sick. It was a constant reminder of the issues I was still plagued by, and I couldn't feel completely free while wearing it. It would constantly lose suction on the wound, triggering an audible beeping alert. The tube itself made a wheezing sound, like a balloon loosing air, when it lost suction on the wound; and to tighten the seal, I had to push on the wound itself, where the wound vac was connected. Once the seal was broken, though, no amount of pushing on that seal would make it fit properly again. Many times, Melinda had to take the entire contraption off of me, clean the wound out, and pack it was gauze and medication. "Packing" is a very accurate description of what had to be done. My wound wasn't like a cut or even a deep gash that just had to be covered. It was still deep enough to put your finger inside of it. Melinda would put some kind of crystals inside the wound that were supposed to keep it clean and fight infection. Next, she would cut chunks of foam into the approximate shape of the wound—it wasn't just straight down either. Toward the bottom, it had a curve to it, which complicated the packing process even more. After the foam was inserted, Melinda had to put padding over the foam to soak up the seepage that came out of the wound after the foam couldn't contain any more of the mess. Over this layer was a layer of extra strong tape that, after being pulled off for a cleaning, left my skin red and irritated. After dealing with this process day-in and day-out and driving an hour to wound care a couple of times each week, I had had enough. I told the staff at the wound therapy center to take the wound vac off—I would no longer be using it. I was cautioned that this would prolong the healing of my back and that the wound might get infected, putting me back in the hospital. I didn't care. I needed it gone. I was done carrying this repulsive thing around that emitted an awful smell and didn't hide the disgusting fluid being pulled through the clear tubing. I had them patch me up and I went home, back to training and hoping that I hadn't made a huge mistake.

With the wound vac gone, I felt a sort of freedom, and I didn't feel as sick as I had before. I also stopped wearing my oxygen throughout the day to train my lungs to deal with the limited oxygen they had to get by on. I always had it on standby, though, and I would monitor my oxygenation level with a small device that I could keep in my pocket. I had learned what were acceptable levels and what were dangerous levels, and I tried to keep it in the correct range.

My appetite was slowly starting to come back as well. Up until this point, I couldn't keep food down for anything. Anytime I ate, I would vomit it back up within minutes, no matter how bland the food was or how slowly I ate it. One time, just to get out of the house, I took Melinda to an Italian restaurant she liked. We thought we would get dressed up a bit and try to have a bit of normalcy. We sat in a booth by the bar so we wouldn't have to wait as long on a table in the main dining area because the restaurant was jam-packed. We were both excited to be out, having a good time. I ordered a salad, and it stayed down well. Feeling confident, I went all-out and got the spicy shrimp with angel hair pasta (my usual). The food came, and I dove into the shrimp. They tasted great! Melinda was enjoying her dish as well. We were having a good time, and I was, surprisingly, feeling okay. I moved onto the pasta and started to couple that with the shrimp when things started to go bad. I felt the now-familiar sensation in my throat, which was almost like a cough coming on. To most people, a cough wouldn't be cause for alarm. In my case, once I started to cough, I would start to hyperventilate, my throat would spasm, my stomach would start to convulse, and I would end up vomiting. Well, I was spot on for this one. The coughing started, and I tried my hardest to keep it at bay. I quickly drank the iced tea I had nearby, which did nothing to help. As the coughing got more and more intense, I felt my stomach start to turn. As I began to vomit, I reached for something, anything, to catch it. I should have grabbed the giant salad bowl. That would have made sense. Instead, I picked my plate up and held it to my mouth. I tried to stop it by gritting my teeth, which only made matters worse by building up the pressure in my mouth. And eventually, the pressure did release...everywhere. As luck would have it, the waiter came by about this time to check on how the food was tasting. To say he was shocked would be an understatement. It was almost comical. Trying to save me from great embarrassment in a tightly packed restaurant on a Saturday evening, Melinda told the waiter I had bitten down on a bone in my food, which had caused me to gag and vomit. The waiter was very nice and apologized profusely. He didn't hesitate to clean up the mess and brought me a few wet towels to clean myself up with. He even gave us a voucher for a free meal (which we never used). We quickly left and headed back home. The evening was ruined for Melinda, but she was a great sport about it, and we actually laughed afterwards. What else are you going to do?

One day, things started to change. I started to be able to hold my food down. As a result, more weight began to stick to me, and I started to get stronger as well. I pushed harder in the gym. I was boxing with my friends, as well as getting back into powerlifting.

I was still weak, but I finally started to gain back the sensation I used to have when I trained, that mind/muscle connection. I started to feel the contractions of the muscles as they actually began working again. A good friend of mine who owned an equipment company that fabricated almost all of the equipment I owned surprised me with a new piece of equipment that would help me in my rehab. Melinda had gotten in contact with him, asked him to build it, and surprised me with it late one evening. I also returned to the gym with my powerlifting team, who had supported me so much, and began to train with them again. There was little emotion attached to my arrival. It was simply time to work. I jumped right into my previous role and started lifting. They, of course, kept (and still keep) their eyes on me to make sure I wasn't going to pass out, but they didn't baby me and feel sorry for my condition. I was accountable for my workouts, and if I happened to miss one, I had to make it up to stay on track. Having people around me treat me as they had before was great for my mental healing.

Over the course of several months, I would take my body from a frail shell of itself to a level of strength I didn't have even before I was sick. This wouldn't be a complete healing, though. As I made progress, all people could see was my physical come-back. When I encountered people I hadn't seen in some time since I was truly sick, they showed great support, but didn't have a clue as to what I was going through mentally. No one can go through this kind of journey without developing some mental issues. The first few times I went back to the hospital and saw the staff, I told them how great everything was for me, and everyone would smile and hug me. One day, I went to visit, though, and I didn't tell them how great it was. I told them how badly things sucked for me. They looked confused but listened. How could any of them know? They treated the physical part of my illness, but they never treated the mental part, which, for me, was the harder of the two to fully heal. When things began to go back to normal was when it truly got bad. Part of me wished I had just died in the hospital. Everything seemed so bland now. Whether what I had experienced when I was unconscious was just a reaction to the drugs or whether I actually saw heaven and hell, no one can tell me. I have to formulate my own ideas on that, and I have. Those visions were enough to make things in this world seem less than inspiring. Things here just seemed pointless and bland, and that made it damn hard to find enjoyment in life.

BACK TO WORK

IT WAS JULY OF 2014, and Melinda and I had decided to travel to Galveston for a little weekend getaway. With all the stress she had been under, she needed some relaxation time, and what she loved best was to go to the pier at the beach and fish. We spent a couple of days just taking it easy, enjoying the warm temperatures and good seafood. We went on a dolphin watch, which I had never done before. We went to a few museums and hung out on the beach. In the evenings, we would go to the pier, rent a couple of fishing poles, and buy bait. Melinda had been going to Galveston for years, staying in the same hotel and fishing off the same pier. I was glad to be part of her tradition, although I was also a bit nervous to see if I could grip the fishing pole tightly enough to keep from launching it out to sea.

One warm, breezy night, we gathered our supplies from the store, went out onto the pier, and settled into a nice spot about halfway down the pier. We set up our chairs, put out our drinks, and started to defrost and cut the bait. In my head, I began to go over the physical act of casting. I hadn't been fishing in years, let alone with my new physical challenges that would, at the very least, make the casting motion awkward. I let Melinda go first. Of course, her line sailed out into the air for what seemed like a hundred yards. Now it was my turn. I grabbed the end of the fishing pole as tightly as I could, extended my arm back, and threw with all my might. My line went out smoothly but dropped probably ten feet from the pier. We looked at each other and laughed. At least I didn't lose the pole over the edge. With the pressure of that first cast off of me, the process became smoother and easier as the night went on. I am very grateful for how quickly my muscle memory returned. Like riding a bike, old, familiar actions soon came back to me.

Melinda and I both caught a number of fish that evening, but I had the biggest haul of the trip. I'm not sure what kind of fish it was, but it was big—big enough for the people around us to come over and watch. I got the fish out of the water and was trying to reel him in. The fish was so big that the fishing pole began to jam. No matter what I did or how many times I cranked on the handle, I couldn't take in any more line. A man, who had brought over a big net and had been giving me instructions, told me to adjust the crank on the pole. I guess I didn't make the adjustment quickly enough, and while I had the fish suspended in the air above the water, the line snapped and the fish made his getaway. So technically, I didn't "catch" the fish because that would have required me to have actually gotten him over the railing and off the hook, but not being an actual fisherman, I'll take credit for the catch.

On our last day in Galveston, Melinda and I had just finished visiting an aquarium and were taking a break on a bench outside when my phone rang. It was the deputy chief of the police department where I had been employed. To be honest, I was kind of nervous about answering it. Everyone at the police department had been so supportive during my stay in the hospital and directly after coming home. At first, someone came by the house almost every day to see how I was doing. As time went on, as could only be expected, they had gone back to their normal lives and routines. No one had been by the house in a while, and I had concentrated on my healing. I let the phone call from the deputy chief go to voicemail. When I heard the tone that a message had been left, I quickly hit the button to listen. The message said that one of the detectives had decided to go back to patrol, and I was next on the list. Before I had gotten sick, I had tested for the position of detective and had scored third out of all the applicants. At the time of the test, there was only one opening, which was filled with the person who had scored highest, but the list was kept active for six months to a year. A few months later, there had been an opening for the number two person. Now, due to one of the detectives leaving, my name had come up. The police department wanted me to start back to work on light duty on Monday. When an officer gets injured and cannot perform his normal duties but is still able to come to work and perform other necessary tasks, light duty allows the officer to get his hours and heal at the same time. I was excited about the message but also, admittedly, a bit scared. I had been out of work for around seven months; I wasn't sure if I was ready to go back to work. I also wasn't sure if I wanted to go back to work as a detective. During my time off, I had longed for what I used to do: patrol work. To *decide* to leave a position is one thing, but to be told you can no longer perform the duties of a position is another. I had been told since I woke up that I would never work patrol again. This lit a fire in me that pushed me to work even harder on my recovery. I had spoken to my patrol sergeant multiple times about returning to work, and he had offered to put me in a squad car with another officer for safety to see what I could still physically do. If I got tired, the other officer would take over for me and I could rest. I was so thankful to have a sergeant that would make those accommodations for me. How many supervisors would make that kind of offer?

Patrol officers are broken into shifts, each with its own supervisor. Each officer is responsible for a pre-determined sector, handling all the calls for that area. We rely heavily on each officer coming to work and fulfilling his responsibilities so another officer doesn't have to carry his own work and another officer's work as well. When this does happen, due to illness or a vacation, it makes for a very stressful workday for everyone else. My sergeant was willing to keep me on his shift and not take on another officer (which he was offered). My shift mates also had decided to keep my spot open. This was a huge honor they had given me and showed the highest levels of respect. Now I was faced with the choice of going back to work in a position I had aspired to, while letting down all of my buddies on my patrol shift who had been holding my spot open for me, or returning the respect they had shown me and going back to work with them. If I didn't take the detective position, though, I would be passing up a great opportunity I had aimed for, prior to getting sick.

I sat with Melinda on that bench and talked over the dilemma at length. In the end, for my healing and for everything I had worked for prior to getting sick, I decided to take the position as detective. I called the deputy chief back and told him I would come back to work on Monday as a detective. It took a while for me to get up the nerve, but then I placed a phone call to my patrol sergeant and told him what I would be doing, starting Monday. There wasn't a long discussion about it. He congratulated me on getting my detective spot, and we hung up. I felt like crap the rest of the day, like I had let him down and slapped everyone in the face who had taken on double the workload while I was gone by keeping my spot open; but in the end, I felt like I had made the right decision.

My first assignment Monday didn't involve sitting at a desk and pushing around papers. Instead, I was instructed to report to the range where firearms training was conducted and to assist the instructors who were putting the entire department through its semi-annual pistol and rifle qualifiers. As far as I could tell, no one knew that I would be at the range that week. Throughout the day, officers would come in groups of five or seven, and I would be standing there to help check in weapons and prepare them for their qualification tests. It was a great chance to see basically everyone in the department and be able to thank them for their support.

Over the course of the next few weeks, I settled into my role as a detective but was still on light duty. I couldn't interact with citizens, at least not in person. I was given cases to file that required limited investigation. At most, I could call someone on the phone to corroborate a story, then complete the necessary paperwork and send the case to the courts. It wasn't the most intriguing work, but I was thankful for it. I didn't have to get up at 3:30 a.m. anymore to get ready for work. I didn't have to put on a polyester/wool uniform and thirty pounds of gear for a twelve-hour shift out in the elements. I could wake up at 5:00 a.m., get dressed in a pair of slacks and a polo, put on my gun and badge, and drive to the office to sit at a desk for ten hours. Compared to what I had been doing for the previous ten years on patrol, it was a vacation, and it allowed me to take my time healing. I could eat whenever I felt like it. If I needed to walk outside to take a break because, mentally, I was having issues, I could do that. But most importantly to me, I could use the restroom whenever I needed to and could take as long as necessary. I know this may seem strange to most people, but when you're a patrol officer on the street, a bathroom break is a luxury that you might not have time for during an entire shift. I remember once literally running from my patrol car, past shoppers, to the bathroom inside a convenience store. When I exited about twenty seconds later, I was moving just as fast to get back into my squad car to handle another incoming call. To get out of uniform with all of your gear on to actually sit for any length of time is not an option. You can be given a call anytime unless you show yourself unavailable for calls, which will screw over your sector mates, and I certainly never wanted to do that. Consequently, I would go only when calls allowed, which wasn't always possible. Now, being able to head to the restroom, take my time, and get back to my desk without a radio on my hip blowing up with calls was foreign to me but was a great change. Going to lunch without checking with a supervisor or seeing how many calls were currently holding (which would kill your lunch plans in an instant and leave you headed to the next call hungry) was also a nice change. Most people don't realize that many cops go whole twelve-hour shifts without getting to stop for a break, let alone an actual meal. I was told a long time ago that, as an officer, it's a privilege to stop and eat and shouldn't be expected...and they were right.

[14]

MY NEW REALITY

WHEN YOU'RE in the hospital, you aren't told that you might come out different, mentally. They tell you a lot about your physical condition. They can give you an estimation of how long it will take you to recover. They can tell you what pills to take to make the pain go away or, at least, be manageable. If you are sick enough, they can even tell you when you might pass away. But they don't tell you how things will be for you mentally.

I left the hospital to high-fives, crying staff members, and people telling me that things would be all downhill now. When I got better, I had speaking engagements to go to because I was considered so special. I gave a speech to a room filled with hundreds of medical professionals, afterwards receiving a standing ovation. People had their pictures taken with me and gifts were given to me just for surviving. I was even honored at a basketball game and taken out to center court to receive an award. I watched the game with a group of close friends in a fancy private suite inside the event center, complete with valet parking and a catered dinner. Everyone told me how lucky I was to be alive and how blessed I was and how everything in my life must be so great now. But it wasn't. My life was far from great. Things had begun to break down. Slowly at first but with gaining momentum, my life started to spiral downward to a point where everything came unglued for me. It wasn't that I didn't appreciate the support and encouragement. In fact, I was blown away when people told me how my experience changed their lives. I was blown away by the gifts people wanted to give me and what they did to honor me, all because of what I went through. I won't say a bad word about any of those people. They meant well. They thought, as many people do—even as I did at the time—that after such an experience, everything would be okay once the ordeal was over. In reality, my situation actually became worse.

It started slowly. One of the earliest times I remember getting upset post-hospital was once when Melinda and I were sitting on the front porch of our house. I loved sitting out there. It was peaceful. I loved to sit outside with a cold beverage and just watch things go by. Or nothing go by...just sit and watch. I liked watching the clouds move through the sky, not noticing anything in particular about them...just watching. It was relaxing for me. Early one afternoon, Melinda and I were both sitting on the front porch, and I caught myself looking at the neighbor's house across the street. There was nothing particularly interesting about the house. It was the usual two-story brick house with a two-car garage and a front porch—the same as half of the houses in our neighborhood. Yet something struck me as funny about the house, and I began to get upset. I use the term "upset" because I don't want to say that I started crying. As would be expected, Melinda moved closer to me and asked me what the matter was. All I could do was point to the house. She began to look around. Was there something she wasn't seeing? No, nothing that would cause a person to instantly break into tears. All I could do was point and cry. It was the texture of the neighbor's house. The freaking texture (!) had sent me into tears. As I looked at the house, I was thrust back into my coma and into the nightmares I had experienced. My memories from that time come and go. Sometimes I perceive a fleeting glimpse that I can't quite grasp. A sound, a scent, or even something as simple as a specific color can trigger my remembrance. Like a dream, I have it for a minute, and then it's gone. Sometimes, though, I can remember the incident so vividly that I get upset. This was one of those times. I wasn't having a bad day prior to this. I was going along as usual, and it just kind of snuck up on me. I sobbed—literally sobbed—for minutes without being able to stop. I'm not talking about some tears rolling down my face. I'm talking about shoulders-shaking, head-in-your-hands, snot-coming-out-your-nose crying. And all I could do was point at the house. How do you explain that to someone? I know Melinda was concerned but also frustrated with me. It made no sense. Why would someone who rarely got upset suddenly break into a sobbing session over the texture of a house? And I couldn't explain it to her; there was no way for her to get it without having had a similar experience. Did I die and go toward a light like many people have described? No, I didn't. Did I see dead relatives who told me everything was going to be okay but it wasn't my time yet? No. I don't know how much of that kind of thing I can actually believe. What I saw was very different—some of it amazing and some of it absolutely terrifying. I know at one point I flat-lined for over a minute in the hospital, but how much time does that equate to on the other side? Who knows? I realize that some of what I remember from being in a coma was probably drug-induced, but I'm not dumb enough to question that part of what I went through, part of what I saw and experienced, is what is on the other side, waiting for me. Some of the experiences I had when I was in the coma I have kept to myself. When I recall some of these memories, they bring about feelings that I don't ever want to have again. At times, when I get a flashback of something terrible that I experienced—even if just for a brief period of time—it can be an awful thing to remember.

Getting upset is frustrating; so is dealing with new emotions when it comes to friends. It would make sense that the people who were around you, supporting you the most when you were down and out, would be friends for life and you would savor every moment with them. Things change, though. Sometimes, your perception of attitudes and motivations can change. Paranoia can set in. Things people do can be taken out of context or misperceived, and no matter how crazy it may seem, that is your reality. People who used to call your wife for updates when you were unable to use the phone continue to call her, even though you are better now. Because of these new dynamics in your relationships, you become isolated. The only advice I can give to a friend of someone who has been through a traumatic experience is to ask them what they need. Little things can affect someone so greatly, in either a good or a bad way. After undergoing trauma, a person may become paranoid, jealous, violent, or more removed and depressed. There is a good chance they may become all of the above, and if they do not find an outlet or a way to deal with these issues it will consume them and destroy everything around them. They have to find a way to cope with the issues in their mind.

Multiple neurologists tested me and told me that my brain scan looked like that of someone who had come back from a war. This was probably the best news I could have received. The way the doctors described how a person with my brain scan might act or perceive things was spot on, and it was wonderful to find out that I wasn't actually crazy but had something that could be managed if I decided to face it and work on it.

I've had a few frank talks with some friends to clear the air about how I had perceived certain actions. I've always been a fan of being open and up-front with people. I don't like to play games, and I feel that, even if someone might get offended, it's better to be honest about what is causing an issue. Did I ruin some friendships by bringing up my concerns? Possibly. If the tables had been turned, I know I would have felt offended if others accused me of the actions I was suggesting they committed. I tried to explain what I was going through so that they might be more understanding in case my accusations were wrong. But I had to confront the issues to get past them. Bottling things up is probably the worst thing for anyone in similar circumstances. As most popular self-help programs teach, acknowledging that you have a problem is the first step in fixing the problem. In a friendship, that mentality might be good enough to repair the relationship, but in a marriage, it might not be enough to fix it. I would find that out soon enough.

I don't know how many times the subject of divorce has come up between Melinda and me since I've gotten out of the hospital, but it's been too often. When the severity of our situation hits me, it wakes me up to a new challenge I need to face to make myself a better person. One of my first major challenges was coming off of my pain medications. The challenges I face in my relationships, especially with Melinda...well, it seems like my paranoia and jealousy play a big role in a lot of it. Being a big, strong guy, able to fulfill the role of husband/boyfriend, makes you feel good. Your wife or girlfriend looks at you in a way that makes you feel confident, like she trusts you to protect her and take care of her. Take away that ability, though, and combine it with an already-growing jealousy, and it can ruin a relationship. For example, at a get-together with friends, a guy asked if I wanted a drink, to which I replied no. He then asked my wife if she wanted something to drink, to which she said yes. He walked a good distance for the drink, and instead of coming back with one for her and one for him, he only had a drink for her. I guess, in the "normal" person's mind, no offense was committed. The guy was just trying to be nice, knowing I had been sick. To me, though, it came across disrespectfully. Some other guy just took care of my wife, and my wife didn't seem to have a problem with it! It's not some other guy's job to get my wife a drink; it's my job! This led to a huge fight between Melinda and me. She could not understand where I was coming from. To go from the guy who takes care of everything for his wife to a sick guy who can't even take care of himself and now has other men taking care of his wife for him—it was enough to send me over the edge! I've been told that this is a crazy way to think or that I'm overreacting. To me it's completely reasonable because *I* would never do that to another man—make him feel like he can no longer handle things for himself or his family. How could other people not see that this type of "assistance" might cause an issue?

From what I've been told, part of my issue now is misinterpreting actions, hearing things that weren't said, or reading unintended meaning into things. Issues started to arise with friends who continually texted my wife. I was assured that nothing inappropriate was going on. In my mind, though, this was disrespectful and out of line. I began to think: *Is it me? Am I really off-kilter from what a "normal" person would think? Am I really overreacting? Would I have gotten angry over this kind of thing before I got sick?* I started to second-guess myself on everything. When was I right while others were wrong? It seemed like I was always wrong now. I could no longer trust my perception of reality, and now my wife, whom I love more than anything, was talking about leaving. "It's too much," she said. Too much. She wanted the confident guy back that she fell in love with. How am I not confident? I'm simply trying to keep people from acting inappropriately toward my wife! Am I just supposed to let people get by with being disrespectful?

I have tried medication to calm my mind but that just turns me into a zombie. Melinda has told me that I'm distant again and don't seem to care about anything anymore. How do I find a middle ground? How do I pretend that certain things don't bother me? How do I control this without doping myself up? I know that she is not happy either. She is not happy with who she is with now, which really gives me a reason to worry. I know this is real from what she tells me. She has looked at apartments to move into to get away from me. To think: the person who was with me through the roughest time of my life and who said she would stay with me even if I were a vegetable might not be around much longer because my attitude has changed. That illustrates how difficult it is to deal with someone with my issues. I think getting help is the biggest step. It's one thing to acknowledge you have a problem, but actually searching out a doctor/counselor, making an appointment, and showing up for it —that takes some dedication. Although I've seen a few doctors and counselors, what has helped me the most is religion. Many people will start to roll their eyes about now. That's fine. For some, seeing a doctor or counselor would be enough. For me, though, if I'm going to be honest, turning to God and people who know God has helped me the most.

I've been a Christian since I was a little kid. I accepted Jesus Christ into my heart when I was at a Bible study for kids in New Jersey, where we used to live. I don't have many memories from when I was little, but for some reason, this one stays with me. Even though I was young, I knew what I was doing, and I felt like I was doing something important that I really believed in. The mistake I made, though, like I'm sure many people make when they are saved, is that I didn't give myself fully to God. I thought being a good person was good enough. I didn't lie, steal, or cheat. I helped people out when they needed it. I was a good friend to those around me, and I was as honest as I could be. I even prayed and went to church. But I was missing the most important part of it all and never saw it. I didn't have a relationship with God. I never bothered to really talk to him, and I certainly never listened —not on a consistent basis, at least. Sure, when I really needed something I would turn to him, but not consistently. I now see how awful that was of me. It had been explained to me many times, but it had never really sunk in. God isn't just a being to pray to when we are in trouble, just as a parent raising a child doesn't want the child to come to them only in times of trouble. It's the same with God—a relationship must be formed. God has many blessings awaiting us, but he wants us to be ready to receive those blessings. He wants us to be mature enough to know how to properly handle them. If we are not living correctly, though, many times, we will not receive those blessings. I believe God gave me a huge opportunity to correct my actions. From what I saw when I was in a coma, I could have easily been taken and I would be dead right now. I saw a battle for my soul that haunts me to this day. God has something for me to accomplish. I know I haven't fully lived up to the promises I made in exchange for God sparing my life. It is difficult sometimes, but I believe commit-ments must be kept. If you say you're going to do something, then you need make your best effort to do it. That's a big problem for many people and why many get stuck in the same unchanging loop of life. Opportunities arise that can open doors to great things if we would only walk through them. Too often, though, we choose to close the door because the great unknown on the other side can be scary. Even if we don't like our current situa-tion, at least we take comfort in the familiarity and in knowing what to expect. I saw people every day in rehab who only gave enough effort to keep from sliding backwards in their healing. They wouldn't put forth the extra effort to get to the next level. Because I broke all expectations, I was seen as someone special, but there isn't anything special about me. I'm far from special. I'm average, at best, but my attitude is different than many people's attitudes. I become obsessed with things. I became obsessed with progress. I get obsessed with out-performing other people. That's what helped me in my rehabilitation. I may not always carry that same attitude into every single thing I do. If I did, then I would be a huge success at this point in my life. What I have done is channel that drive into the things that matter most to me, and I've become the best I can be in these areas of my life.

When I first started powerlifting I became obsessed. I read every article about the sport I could find. I watched every video I could find on the internet. I watched the videos during down time at work or while sitting on the couch at home, when other people were watching movies. I went over technique any chance I could, and I practiced all of the time. During briefings at the police department, I would sit down in a squat stance to mimic doing a box squat, then when briefing broke for the beginning of the shift, I would explode up, using my hamstrings like I was completing a squat. If anyone noticed they would have laughed at me, but I was always trying to improve myself. I even built some of my own equipment to use at the house to put in extra work outside of the gym. I used this same focus and obsession in my rehabilitation. I was always thinking about what I could do to help myself get better faster: another exercise or a different way to do an exercise that would improve my balance, strength, or dexterity. I realize this is what I need to do to get the most out of my marriage. This is also the mentality I need to form a better relationship with God.

When I was sick and trying to get better and I actually gave one-hundred percent, I got results. It's amazing what happens when we really give our all. I also saw what happened when I only gave fifty, sixty, or even ninety percent. The difference was startling! I'd venture to say hardly any of us really put this amount of effort into what we are doing to succeed. I'm reminded of a speaker I listen to on a regular basis. He said that when we want to succeed as badly as we want to breathe then we'll be successful. I've felt the fear of wanting to breathe over anything else in this world. It was probably the scariest moment of my life. To know that, in seconds, death would come and take me away, and there was nothing I could do to stop it—that was a powerful feeling; and being able to tap into that feeling and relate it to other activities is something that many people can't do. But if a person can harness that need, that desire, then I believe almost anything in the world is open to them, no matter what the goal. It's the desire to do great things and the ability to follow through that make the unthinkable possible. Hold yourself accountable for what happens to you and how you react. Do the things other people aren't willing to do. Go through the pain that comes with breaking through barriers and, eventually, those barriers will fall.

I thought getting sick and trying to recover would be the biggest challenge of my life. Months in a coma; months of physical therapy and building my body back up; coming off of pain meds; or maybe dealing with the emotional and mental strain in the aftermath: none of these hurdles were my biggest challenge. My biggest challenge was coming to terms with the fact that I wasn't living how I was supposed to be living and making the changes that needed to be made. Breaking down and realizing that I need to submit to what God wants me to do: that was the biggest challenge and maybe the reason for all of the events that took place. My sickness was simply the final tipping point for me to completely break down and be at my lowest.

I believe that things—good and bad—happen for a reason. My sickness and the trials I have been through happened for a reason. There is something for me to learn from this experience, and I believe that I'm supposed to help other people who have similar issues and are having trouble coping. I know the support structure and coping skills I have developed through my job and upbringing aren't typical, so I can only imagine what others who don't possess these skills are going through in similar circumstances. I have to believe that is why many people get hooked on pain medication or commit suicide. There simply isn't an adequate system in place to help once inpatient treatment has either slowed down or ended. I stay motivated to push forward, knowing that tomorrow always brings a chance to start over again, a chance to try and climb that mountain again. But the greatest relief of all is to know that I am loved and accepted by God, and he will be by my side, no matter how bad things get. I can always count on that.

It wasn't too long ago when things seemed so dark. If I had given up then I would not have the blessings I have now. I know I have to keep pushing forward with my dreams and goals, one step at a time, because we never really know how close we are to achieving them or what tomorrow might bring.

Things still aren't ideal for Melinda and me, but I believe, if I continue to try, things will work out. For God to restore my body to what it was before was a blessing beyond belief. There is no medical explanation for my full recovery. It has all been part of God's plan, and I have come to realize that I need to listen to Him. I've been given a chance not many people are given, and I'm going to make the most of it.

ACKNOWLEDGMENTS

This book is dedicated to all of those who have supported me through this journey: my parents, Jo Ann and Mike Gonzalez, who were at my bedside many days and nights; my sisters, Colette and Crissy, who always had kind words for me and encouraged me during my rehab at the hospital or from hundreds of miles away, talking to me over the phone; all of my brothers and sisters at the police department who spent hours outside my room watching guard, sitting by my bedside, praying, and supporting me through fundraisers to help with medical bills; my weightlifting family (Bad Attitude Gym, Physical FX Studio, Black Iron Barbell) who also helped with fundraisers and also kept watch over me in the hospital; those who helped with my rehab and getting back to the gym and training when I needed motivation and to be treated normally again (Nic Tuttle, Scott Proseck, Clint Grams, Jeff Capps, and Sean Donegan); those friends who waited outside my room for hours when I was having surgery or an unscheduled treatment just to spend a short amount of time with me, or were turned away because my condition had worsened (Driver, Brunson, Goodman, Bastida, Hobbs);

too many medical staff to name that saved my life many times over and put in hours and hours by my side to give me chance after chance when things looked darkest; most importantly, though, my wife and love, Melinda. This book is dedicated to you. You have gone through more suffering during this process than I have and are still suffering to this day—you have to deal with the after-effects of my changed personality and emotions that no one else has to see. You are a true warrior who keeps her head high and soldiers forward. I am just a survivor in all of this. I love you...thank you, Melinda.

PICTURES OF ME

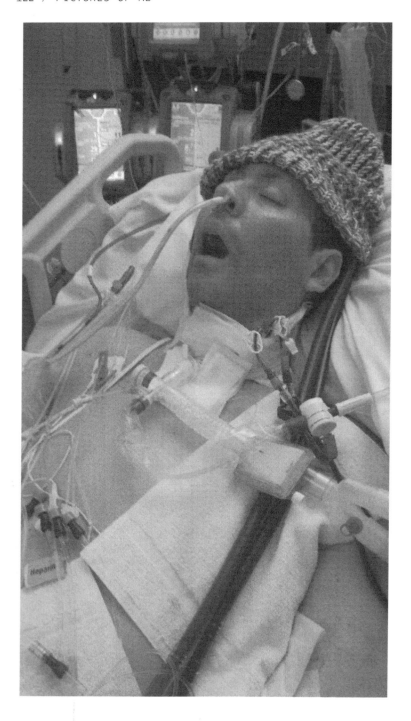

Made in the USA
San Bernardino, CA
26 January 2019